The Albertans

100 People Who Changed the Province

FIRST EDITION CONTRIBUTORS

Ken Bolton
Sharon A. Fogarty
Donaleen Saul
Sheonaid Ursan
Jean Crozier
R.R. Kennedy
Elaine Trimble

SECOND EDITION CONTRIBUTORS

Ken Davis
Scott Rollans

Lone Pine Publishing

© 2005 by Lone Pine Publishing
First printed in 2005   10 9 8 7 6 5 4 3 2 1
Printed in Canada

The Publisher: Lone Pine Publishing

10145–81 Avenue
Edmonton, AB Canada, T6E1W9
Website: www.lonepinepublishing.com

1808–B Street NW , Suite 140
Auburn, WA USA, 98001

Library and Archives Canada Cataloguing in Publication
    The Albertans : 100 people who changed the province / Ken Bolton ... [et al.]. - Rev. and updated ed.

Includes index.
ISBN 13: 978–1–55105–511–4
ISBN 10: 1-55105-511-2

1. Alberta--Biography. I. Bolton, Ken, 1943-

FC3655.A42 2005   920.07123   C2005-904152-8

Editorial Director: Nancy Foulds
Project Editor: Sandra Bit
Photo Coordinator: Carol Woo
Production Manager: Gene Longson
Design & Layout: Heather Markham
Cover Design: Elliot Engley, Curtis Pillipow, Gerry Dotto

PC: P5

Table of Contents

Acknowledgements

The first edition of this book was a 75th anniversary project in 1980, and was made possible by Alberta Education. *The Albertans* was developed by the Alberta Compendium Project Committee, whose members all gave generously of their several and varied talents to design and make the novel project a success. Their selection of 75 names from more than 300 suggested by interested groups and individuals throughout the province was a difficult and unenviable task.

In the ensuing 25 years, Alberta has undergone many changes, challenges and successes, and a new freshness is permeating the province in 2005. It seemed appropriate, then, to celebrate Alberta's 100th anniversary by revising and expanding Lone Pine's first edition of *The Albertans*, published in 1981. In addition to updating the stories of those individuals from the first edition whose contributions to the greatness of the province of Alberta continued, we've added new and important province builders from the last 25 years and shared their stories.

Choosing who to include in the new section was very difficult; out of many possibilities, we tried to select individuals who reflect the province's contemporary diversity, the industrial and the artistic, the philanthropic and the scientific. In the process, many notable Albertans, whose contributions were no less important, had to be left out. We regret that there are many whose stories we did not have room for.

We would also like to acknowledge the fine and dedicated work of those involved in creating the first edition.

Thank you

Preface to the Second Edition

The Albertans originally was published in 1981: it was a project celebrating the province's 75th birthday and the first book ever published by Lone Pine Publishing. A blue-ribbon committee selected 75 Albertans who were deemed particularly notable, and the book was an assemblage of biographies of those so chosen.

Twenty-five years later, Alberta is marking its 100th anniversary as a province, and Lone Pine has published hundreds of books. It seems an appropriate time to update *The Albertans*, this time featuring 100 remarkable human beings who have called this province home at one time or another.

We have drawn the additional people largely from those who came to prominence over the past quarter-century. We have sought to reflect the diversity of race, gender and profession that is at the heart of Alberta's rich cultural and economic life.

Alberta has been transformed from a wilderness on the northern edge of the Great Plains to a modern, sophisticated society in the amazingly short span of 100 years. From sodbusters to oil rig crews to the builders of cities, generation after generation of Albertans have committed to building something better. Today many Albertans make their contribution not only at home but on a world stage, acclaimed for excellence wherever they go. As a people, we are innovative and fearless about dreaming big.

The 25 years since *The Albertans* was first written have seen tremendous changes in this province. Edmonton and Calgary have grown to cities of a million each in population while another four cities now have populations in excess of 50,000 people. This underscores Alberta's continuing and intense shift to an urban versus a rural population.

Alberta's economy has made significant strides in diversification, particularly in such fields as medicine and communications. Oil still is the dominant economic engine, with the tar sands of northeastern

Alberta having emerged as a multibillion-dollar industry unto itself. With an end to easily accessible oil and gas fields in sight, the province is moving to build a knowledge-based economy that will have strength when the energy resources are depleted. Alberta has seen a recent explosion in the number of post-secondary institutions providing education and job training throughout the province.

Ethnic diversity has intensified significantly over the past quarter-century. Alberta now boasts substantial communities originating in nations around the world. The newcomers have brought new cultures, faiths and values with them, enriching the perspective of all who live here.

Politically, Alberta has been somewhat anomalous, appearing on the surface to have remained unchanged or increasingly reactionary in its conservatism of the past 30 years. Within the ruling Conservative Party, however, there was certainly movement; from the culturally expansive and urban party of Peter Lougheed to the post-recession government that brought cutbacks and extensive privatization of government services under Ralph Klein.

Over the past 25 years, Albertans have demonstrated an immense spirit of innovation and commitment when it comes to building a diverse and vibrant artistic community. The province has become known as the summer festival centre of the continent, with classical, jazz, folk, blues, bluegrass and a wide array of ethnic festivals coming one after another over the province's all too brief summer. Alberta is home or place of origin to a sizable community of recording artists who enjoy a worldwide or national following: k.d. lang, Jann Arden, Paul Brandt, Ian Tyson, Corb Lund, Bill Bourne, Amanda Forsyth, Carolyn Dawn Johnson, Terry Clark and many more.

Edmonton has a new world-class concert hall while Calgary boasts the massive Epcor Centre for the Performing Arts. Symphony, opera, ballet, modern dance, theatre: it's all there and performed to the highest standards found anywhere.

Edmonton and Calgary also are emerging as important "smart" cities, where higher learning and advanced research are vital industries in themselves. Calgary, aside from being the energy capital of the country, is home to more corporate head offices than any other English-speaking Canadian city except Toronto. In Edmonton, the University of Alberta has developed medical research facilities that are second to none on the continent, and its researchers regularly contribute significant achievements in the treatment of cancer, diabetes and other diseases.

Among the hundreds of thousands of hard-working, intelligent Albertans who have built this province brick by brick, some have emerged who are extraordinary for their talent, insight, leadership or humanity. We humbly offer this collection of stories about 100 such Albertans, knowing full well there are many deserving candidates left unheralded but no less worthy. This book is for all of them.

Introduction to the First Edition: Before 1905

by John Patrick Gillese

Just over 110 years ago, the wife of Methodist minister George L. McDougall watched with eyes that could weep no more as her husband and one son, David, buried her two daughters and another son's wife (all victims of a smallpox epidemic) in the mission graveyard at Pakan, 70 miles downriver from Fort Edmonton.

"It is a hard thing," her son said as they filled in the earth, "to bury our own dead."

It was part of the price paid to open up the West.

Hardship, loneliness and danger were no strangers to the first Albertans.

Not to Peter Pond, caulking his canoes with tarry sand where Fort McMurray stands today.

Not to Father Lacombe, dodging Cree and Blackfoot bullets 13 years after he had vowed to spend his life to bring peace to "the children of the plains," and whose love for them proved greater than their hate for each other.

Not even to someone like "Slippery Annie," who stars in the colourful folklore of southern Alberta as the woman who finally got her husband-to-be to show up for their wedding—dead drunk. "Bring him back when he's sober!" ordered the appalled clergyman. "The trouble is," poor Annie responded, "he won't come when he's sober."

Few of those who came West before Alberta was a province were as colourful as Jerry Potts, the bandy-legged scout for the North-West Mounted Police, or John Ware, the famous Black cowboy. But in a less dramatic way they were as rugged and independent as Billy Henry who, at the age of almost 100, was finally induced to enter a senior citizens' home, only to take off the next morning for his cabin near High River. His reason for leaving? "Too danged many old people in that place."

In preparing this book about famous Albertans, some 326 personalities were formally considered: explorers, missionaries, traders, ranchers, farmers, lawmakers (perhaps even a few lawbreakers, most of whom led exemplary lives in this province where people could bury their past, could build their own future).

Space, for one thing, precluded the possibility of featuring more than a select few. Additionally, all occupants and all decades of our history had to be represented. Hence, the major portion of this book has been given over to the history of Alberta since its inception as a province—and those who made that history.

The life stories of many more—known and unknown, colourful, or of the steady stuff on which lasting progress is built—remain a rich human historical resource to be researched and written by our authors, who themselves may be descendents of these pioneers. The point is: every land needs its heroes, and this work is designed to acknowledge the debt we owe to so many, the unnamed as surely as the famed.

In such debt, Alberta is rich. Where explorers and missionaries lit their campfires, our cities stand golden in the sun today. The character, the courage, the ideals of those who opened up our West live on today in the excellence and achievements of their children and grandchildren. The interdependence of neighbours—whose unfailing asset was the sure help of one another through good times and bad—brought into being a singularly united and warm-hearted people whose way of life is the envy of much of the world.

The death of the Reverend George McDougall, in a way, typifies all those, known and unknown, whose lives are touched on in this book—but especially those courageous first settlers who put down roots that have made Albertans strong, proud and independent to the present day.

The elder McDougall died on a buffalo hunt in January 1876— when the old West was ending and a new Alberta was soon to be born. Alone, separated from his son John and their small hunting party, he knew death was coming in the bitter sub-zero cold, and he met it as he had met every other challenge of his lifetime. When his body was found, it was laid out as if for burial.

"His work was finished," said his son at the funeral.

Only in a sense.

In another sense, it had only begun.

That faith, courage and greatness of heart of all our early settlers lives on in the way of life that makes Alberta the good land it is today.

—J.P.G.

February 1981

1905—

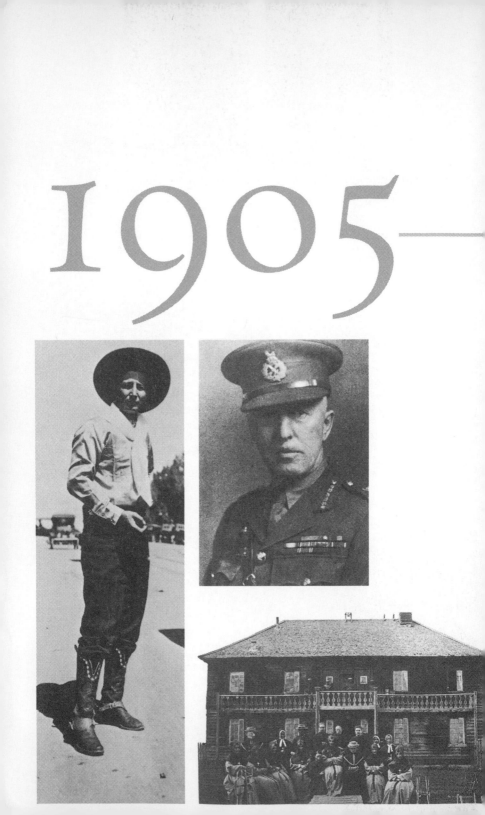

1918

As They Sow

The North-West Rebellion was a generation past
and railways had transformed the territory.

In Edmonton
crowds had gathered in the sunshine
of an early September morning.

Alberta was to be proclaimed a province—
the eighth in the Dominion of Canada.
A territory had come of age.

A.C. Rutherford

Alberta became a province on September 1, 1905. The next day, it had the only provincial premier to be appointed rather than elected.

Alexander Cameron Rutherford had come to Alberta in 1895 after practising law for 10 years in his native Ontario. He quickly became involved in the politics of the North-West Territories. In 1902, he was elected as Strathcona's representative to the Territorial Assembly at Regina. Shortly afterward, he was elected deputy speaker of the Assembly.

In February 1905, Prime Minister Laurier introduced a bill in Parliament to make Alberta a province. It passed, and G.H.V. Bulyea was named as lieutenant-governor. By this time, Alex Rutherford was president of the Alberta Liberal Association, and Lieutenant-Governor Bulyea appointed him the province's first premier. The method of selection was controversial, but a provincial election two months later confirmed Rutherford's position. The Liberals captured 23 seats out of 25.

One of the new government's first acts was to choose Edmonton as permanent capital of the province. This upset many of Rutherford's colleagues from southern Alberta, who favoured Calgary as the capital. As a consequence, Calgarians expected their city to be chosen as the site of the proposed provincial university. But even this honour was denied. The Cabinet decided to establish the university in Strathcona, and Premier Rutherford personally selected the site on the banks of the North Saskatchewan.

Education was a principal interest of Alex Rutherford. He attended the Imperial Conferences on Education in London in 1907 and 1911. He considered the establishment of the University of Alberta his finest achievement as premier.

There were other achievements, of course. He chose the site of the province's legislative building, for which he laid the cornerstone in 1909. His government established the provincial telephone system. He also helped found the Historical Society of Alberta.

Alberta's second provincial election was held in 1909. The Liberals won handily, 37 to 3. They had run under the slogan of "Rutherford, Reliability and Railways."

The "railways" part of that slogan came back to haunt the premier. A generous deal had been worked out between the provincial government and the American owners of the Alberta and Great Waterways Railways. The deal was criticized and a royal commission was appointed to investigate.

Premier Rutherford resigned in 1910 because of the railway scandal and because of bickering within his Cabinet. Some members were still sore about Edmonton being chosen both as the provincial capital and as the home of the university.

The royal commission cleared Premier Rutherford of any wrongdoing but claimed he had failed to act in the best interests of the province. Rutherford was by now bitter about the opposition from within his own party, but ran again for the Liberals in 1913. He was defeated. In 1921, he campaigned for the Conservatives.

Among the honours A.C. Rutherford received during his life were doctorates from several Canadian universities, the King's Jubilee Medal and the title of honorary colonel of the 194th Highland Battalion. The greatest honour came in 1927, when he was appointed chancellor of the university he had founded. He held that position until his death in 1941 at the age of 84.

The Toronto *Globe* once described Alexander Cameron Rutherford as "an honest, upright figure in politics. A big man physically and mentally with a radiant humour in his eyes, and lines of stubborn strength finely blended in his genial face." A political foe who became a personal friend, Prime Minister R.B. Bennett, called him "an honest man, but over his head in politics."

A.C. Rutherford was a lover of books. After his death, most of his fine book collection was given to the University of Alberta. It is now housed in Rutherford Library, named for the man known as the father of both the province and its university. Rutherford House, the Rutherford family home, has been preserved with many of the family's possessions. It is now a historic site on the north side of the campus, overlooking the river.

Frank Oliver

"Honest Frank," as his friends called him, was one of the first people to settle in what is now Edmonton. He was also largely responsible for putting it on the map.

Frank was born in Peel County, Ontario in 1853 and, while completing high school, worked on his father's farm and apprenticed as a printer with the local paper. He had a disagreement with his father and changed his last name from Bowsfield to his mother's maiden name, Oliver. Frank spent the next few years continuing to work as a printer. In 1876, at the age of 23, he was lured west to Edmonton.

Frank Oliver was obviously a man of vision and imagination, because there was nothing alluring or promising about Edmonton at that time. It was a collection of shacks and tents around a trading

post 1600 kilometres from the nearest railway. Frank pitched his tent where the
University of Alberta now stands. Not
intimidated by the mightiness of the
Hudson's Bay Company, he opened a
tiny rival store near the trading giant's
Fort Edmonton. To get his supplies, he
made four hazardous trips to Winnipeg every year.

As Edmonton grew, its people
became interested in keeping in touch
with world events. Frank rose to the challenge and on December 6, 1880, the first
issue of the *Edmonton Bulletin*, a tiny 5-by-7-inch,
two-page weekly went to press.

Edmonton went through a series of booms and busts, but it continued to grow, and Frank Oliver's paper grew along with it. "Read
the Bible and the Bulletin" was its slogan and, in a number of ways,
it served as a manifesto for the settlement and development of western Canada. Frank's editorials lashed out at the powers in Ottawa
who "didn't give a damn" about the needs of westerners.

In the early days of settlement, the federal government was slow
in getting the land surveyed. Some homesteaders were fined or jailed
for selling wood from their land claims They were also vulnerable to
claim-jumpers moving onto their land. Frank was part of a group
who took it upon themselves to push a claim-jumper's shack over
the riverbank. He was arrested, but the jury found him not guilty.

Frank Oliver became the first representative elected to the
North-West Territorial Council. He was responsible for getting the
Territories their school law and election law. He was strongly
opposed "to the North-West being taxed by Ottawa, without being
represented there, and to its local affairs and finances being conducted by Ottawa appointees instead of by the people of this country." For this reason, he chose to run for federal office in 1896. He

was elected to the House of Commons as an independent Liberal, and played a major role in establishing Edmonton as the seat of government for Alberta. He served in Prime Minister Wilfrid Laurier's Cabinet as Minister of the Interior and Superintendent of Indian Affairs.

He was not a handshaker or a baby-kisser, but throughout his 34-year political career, he earned the love and respect of many people. At the time of his death at age 80, he was still "in harness," and working as a member of the Board of Railway Commissioners. Perhaps the best testimony to Frank's faith and courage came from one of his close friends: "There was a man who would always fight for what he considered the right. They couldn't buy him, and they couldn't scare him."

The Grey Nuns

Western Canada in the mid-19th-century, the fur traders would tell you, was "no place for white women, particularly those delicately reared in a convent." However, in 1859, Sister Lamy, Sister Alphonse and Sister Superior Leblanc Emery, stiff and bruised from their 85-day journey from Montreal, climbed out of their Red River cart at Lac Ste. Anne, in what is now Alberta. The first educated white women in western Canada, they belonged to the Institute of the Sisters of Charity, better known as the Grey Nuns.

They arrived in response to a plea from Bishop Provencher, who needed their help in ministering to the needs of the Native and Metis people. The fur trade had brought inter-tribal warfare, illicit liquor traffic and diseases. A single smallpox epidemic in 1869 spread through the North-West like prairie fire, wiping out one-half of the Native population.

The sisters had their work cut out for them, and under extremely inhospitable living conditions. Upon arriving at Lac Ste. Anne, the sisters immediately learned Cree, and 15 days later opened a school for 30 Native students. Many of their students were in their early 20s, the same age as two of the sisters.

The threat of starvation soon made it impossible for them to continue their efforts in Lac Ste. Anne, so they moved to St. Albert, taking seven orphan girls with them. The first convent was a log cabin loaned to them by Father Lacombe, OMI. They set up an orphanage as well as the Youville Residential School, which later expanded to include students from five reserves.

The Grey Nuns' work in St. Albert also included establishing, in 1891, the first hospital, a frame structure attached to the mission. Edmonton was growing rapidly, and diseases such as typhoid and smallpox, as well as pneumonia, blood poisoning and appendicitis, were taking their toll among the population. In 1894, six young doctors asked the Grey Nuns to set up a General Hospital in Edmonton. The sisters moved fast. They purchased land from the Hudson's Bay Company, and two of them lived in a shack on the grounds to oversee the construction. In less than a year, the hospital was ready to receive its first patients.

The activities of the Grey Nuns were not confined to the Edmonton area. They set up hospitals in Calgary, St. Paul, Cardston and Fort McMurray, and Native schools in St. Paul, Cardston, Brocket and Fort Chipewyan. They established missions the full length of Canada, from Aklavik to Chesterfield Inlet; and in the United States, Japan, China, Haiti and Africa.

With new responsibilities, the Grey Nuns moved with changing times. The directorship of their hospitals has passed on to the community. The Grey Nuns continue to serve their communities as social workers, teachers and nurses. The attitude that has guided their labours for centuries still prevails. "Ever on the threshold of want, yet never lacking in the essentials." It's an attitude that humanized the Canadian West.

Henry Marshall Tory

Alberta's first premier, A.C. Rutherford, wanted a university. In 1908, he gave the job of creating it to a remarkable physics professor named Henry Marshall Tory. Classes began that September with 37 students. When Dr. Tory left 20 years later, the University of Alberta had six buildings and over 1600 students.

Henry Marshall Tory was born on the Nova Scotia farm his great-grandfather had received for serving Britain during the American Revolutionary War. After a year of secondary education, he taught in a rural school and later went to McGill University in Montreal.

The life of a scholar and educational pioneer had begun. In 1890, Tory won the university's gold medal in mathematics and physics. He was also active in student activities, especially debating. This Maritime farmboy, whose Scottish ancestors had supported Bonnie Prince Charlie, once defended the beheading of King Charles I in a debate. He presented his case so brilliantly that the subject was considered no longer debatable at McGill. Henry Tory was unanimously chosen top orator of his graduating class.

Next, he took a Bachelor of Divinity degree and spent two years preaching in a Montreal church. In 1893, however, he returned to McGill to lecture in mathematics.

With a doctoral degree in science (1903), Dr. Tory became McGill's roving ambassador. He set up a campus in Vancouver, which later became part of the University of British Columbia. He also helped bring two Maritime colleges, Acadia and Mount Allison, into affiliation with McGill.

Then, for 20 years, his personality dominated the new University of Alberta. Under Dr. Tory, scientific research and adult education became trademarks of the university. He felt it was necessary to "take the university to the people." This same commitment to adult education took him to England to set up Canada's "Khaki College" for veterans of the First World War.

In 1928, Dr. Tory left Alberta to head Canada's National Research Council in Ottawa. It subsequently became one of the world's most important research organizations. In 1942, he took on the task of building another university, Carleton College, in Ottawa. When he became president of Carleton, Dr. Tory was 79!

When Henry Marshall Tory died in 1947, Prime Minister Mackenzie King called him "an outstanding figure in fields of higher education and scientific research and of public service." Perhaps the best assessment of his life came from Dr. Tory himself: "I am a pioneer!"

A.E. Cross

He was 23 years old and, like so many others of his day, he succumbed to the lure of the West. In 1884, Alfred Ernest Cross jumped on the Canadian Pacific Railway and arrived in Calgary— one year after the railway itself. He worked as a bookkeeper, veterinarian and hired hand at a nearby ranch owned by Senator Matthew Cochrane. Having survived the trials of a hard winter and a wet and stormy spring, Cross then decided to strike out on his own.

In 1888, a riding accident proved to be a turning point in his career. His doctor advised him to move to Calgary where medical assistance would be more readily available, so he had to turn his attention to a more urban-oriented enterprise. Cross hit upon the ideal product—beer. For thirsty westerners tired of low-grade rotgut, it was a sure thing. So Cross set about learning everything he could about breweries, studying and acquiring diplomas in Montreal, New York and Chicago. Thoroughly schooled in the art and science of beer production, he founded the Calgary Brewing and Malting Company. His first brew was so well received by the men at the brewery and Mr. Cross's friends that, in "tasting" the batch, they ended up downing the whole lot.

In his heart, however, he remained a rancher. A.E. Cross was active in what became the Western Stock Growers Association. This organization arose because the federal government appeared to be unconcerned with the problems of ranchers, who were experiencing conflicts over land leases and were suffering losses of their herds to wolves and cattle thieves.

In the election of 1899, he ran for the Conservative Party in the East Calgary constituency and won. As a member of the North-West

Territories Legislative Assembly, he was active in the struggle to obtain provincial status for Alberta.

By 1912, the Montreal-born graduate of eastern veterinary and agricultural schools had expanded his land holdings to become the owner of one of the largest ranches in Alberta, the A7. Part of his success was derived from his selection of the choicest varieties of cattle. In 1917, at a fair in Chicago, he received the highest price ever paid in the world market for grass-fed steers.

As a prominent Calgary businessman, Cross had a hand in developing a number of companies, including Canadian Western Natural Gas, Alberta Flour Mills, Royalite Oil and the Royal Trust Company. He was also one of the "Big Four" founders of the Calgary Stampede and a director of the Calgary General Hospital.

Alfred Ernest Cross, through his achievements as pioneer rancher, businessman and politician, was a key figure in the development of both the city of Calgary and the province as a whole.

Bob Edwards

As Bob Edwards once said, "It is well that there is no one without a fault for he would not have a friend in the world." For someone like Robert Chambers Edwards, a Scotsman who arrived in western Canada in 1894, the remark was revealing. He was both saint and sinner—widely admired for his brilliant honesty and despised by others for his lapses into "drunken degeneracy" and "libellous cynicism." Such extremes of character made him an ideal journalist in early Alberta.

The *Wetaskiwin Free Lance* was his first western Canadian paper, and was also the first newspaper between Calgary and Edmonton. Chambers arrived in Alberta after working as a farmhand in Iowa, referring to Wetaskiwin as a place with "287 souls and three total abstainers." He wanted to call the paper the "Wetaskiwin Bottling Works," but his friends advised against it.

Opposition to his outrageous views caused him to move on, first to Leduc and then to Strathcona. There he started *The Alberta Sun*, once again bowing to convention by resisting naming it the "Strathcona Strathcolic." However, it was a difficult time for small-time newspaper editors, and the struggle to keep the tiny paper going proved too much for him.

He therefore departed for Winnipeg and got a job as a staff writer for a daily. But working regular hours and meeting deadlines went against his freewheeling nature, so the rolling stone rolled to High River, in what is now Alberta. There, on March 4, 1902, the *Eye Opener* was born. Bob Edwards' drinking habits and his editorial style soon brought him into conflict with the community's Methodist church. Discouraged, he went to Calgary and, in early 1904, his paper re-emerged as the *Calgary Eye Opener*.

There he finally found an audience who could appreciate the high quality of his writing, his humour and his criticism. He pulled no punches in his attacks on political figures, businessmen and socialites. In many ways, however, he confused his readers. He was officially a Conservative, but was obviously a reformer. He lambasted the Church, but was a believer and practitioner of Christian charity. He was a self-confessed heavy drinker, yet he supported prohibition. It is little wonder that people didn't know what to make of him.

His attacks on public figures did not go down well with his hapless victims, but miraculously he always managed to avoid being sued for libel. Ironically, Eye Opener Bob launched a libel suit of his own against the publisher of Calgary's *Daily News*. Daniel McGillicuddy, with whom Edwards had had a running battle, had published a vindictive attack that hurt him deeply. He enlisted the aid of his lawyer friend, Paddy Nolan, and a suit was launched. The verdict was technically in Edwards' favour, but McGillicuddy got only a small fine and Edwards was reprimanded for publishing "debasing and demoralizing" material in his paper. It was such a disillusioning experience for Edwards that he decided to leave Calgary.

He remained in eastern Canada for two years, but he returned to Alberta in 1911. *The Albertan*, a Calgary newspaper, agreed to publish the *Eye Opener* and once again he was back in business, achieving the biggest circulation west of Toronto, excluding the Winnipeg dailies.

Two significant decisions in his life bore out his tendency to do the unexpected. The first was in 1917 when, at the age of 53, he married—something he had sworn never to do. Bob Edwards declared, "When a man is in love for the first time, he thinks he invented it."

His second uncharacteristic action was to run for political office. He ran as an Independent candidate in the 1921 provincial election and won by a large majority, although he made only one 60-second political speech. A statement he had once made turned out to be a prophecy. "Now I know what a statesman is: he is a dead politician, and what this country needs is more of them." Bob Edwards died in 1922, having served in the legislature for only one year. It is an irony that he would have appreciated.

William Fairfield

He was known as Alberta's agricultural trailblazer. Born in 1867 in Titesville, Pennsylvania, William Harmon Fairfield was in the fifth generation of a family of British settlers who had come to the New World in 1630. Agriculture had a strong appeal for William, and he enrolled at the Colorado State Agriculture College and later at the University of Wyoming, receiving degrees in agriculture and horticulture.

Meanwhile, word of a boom in the Canadian West made its way south of the border, and William and his brother Harry were intrigued by the prospect of testing their knowledge on the frontier farmland. "We just figured the cattle range and irrigation combination was for us," William later reported.

He established a ranch near Lethbridge, which turned out to be a godsend for southern Alberta. He had the education and the expertise to follow through on many of the novel schemes put forth by William Pearce, a land surveyor referred to as the "Father of Southern Alberta Irrigation."

Charles Ora Card, Mormon leader in south-central and northern United States, approached Fairfield with his first challenge. Card's people had been trying unsuccessfully to grow alfalfa in the area. William considered the problem and devised a procedure in which he "inoculated" the Alberta soil with soil from Wyoming upon which alfalfa had been grown successfully. The Alberta Railway and Irrigation Company was so impressed with Fairfield's experiment that it purchased 400 acres for an experimental farm, with Fairfield in charge. Between 1905 and 1945, he devoted himself to the job. Through his efforts, farmers learned to farm effectively using irrigation, to break the land efficiently, to use suitable varieties of seeds and to plant and rotate their crops in a way that would produce the greatest yield. He discovered that adding sulphur to the grey-wooded soils of southern Alberta and Saskatchewan nearly doubled productivity.

Fairfield's work in the expansion of irrigation created a flourishing sugar beet industry in the province. Millions of trees now grace what was once bald prairie because he motivated local farmers to plant windbreaks on their land.

His vast contribution to agriculture earned him acclaim beyond his community, including an honorary doctor's degree from the University of Alberta in 1940. King George VI, in 1953, honoured him with membership in the Order of the British Empire for his service to agriculture and to humanity in general. Three years before his death, in 1961, hundreds of friends, colleagues, agricultural scientists, farmers, ranchers and businessmen gathered to commemorate his receiving of a fellowship in the Agricultural Institute of Canada, the association's highest honour. It was a fitting tribute to a person who could claim to have done more for agriculture in southern Alberta than any other.

Tom Three Persons

When the Calgary Stampede made its debut in September 1912, the public response was overwhelming. Despite continuous and heavy rains, 24,000 spectators were there to enjoy steer roping, bull-dogging, trick ropers and riders. There was a parade of trappers, prospectors, cowboys, Royal North-West Mounted Police troops, buffalo teams, ox-teams and Natives, who completely surrounded the city with their tents and teepees.

It was the first big event for Calgary, and the Canadian cowboys felt at a bit of a disadvantage competing with famous and experienced cowboys from all over the United States. However, there was one competitor that few local cowboys or the visitors had heard of.

His name was Tom Three Persons, a tall, handsome, 25-year-old aboriginal from Standoff on the Blood Reserve. A fine rider, he had been persuaded by his friends to enter the bronco-riding contest. But there was one small hitch. Moments before the contest was to begin, he was languishing in the Royal North-West Mounted Police jail at Fort Macleod for an unrecorded act of public mischief. As good fortune would have it, the Inspector of Indian Agencies made a plea to have Tom released in time to ride, and arranged to have a cash bond posted on his behalf. Tom was rushed to the Stampede Grounds just as the bronco-riding contest was getting underway.

The name of the horse he drew was Cyclone, a bucking, snorting and wild-eyed black demon that had never been successfully ridden by anyone. Even Tom's competitors were sympathetic. Cyclone's trick of rearing wildly, teetering on his hind legs and threatening to throw himself backwards, had caused more than 125 of the world's best cowboys to hit the dirt. But Tom seemed unperturbed and his instincts told him that Cyclone was too clever to actually fall over, so he called the horse's bluff. Three Persons stayed on as Cyclone reared and spun and flipped from one end of the arena to the other. It was a ride to the finish, the first ever.

Bedlam broke out in the stands. A crowd surrounded Three Persons, congratulating him, for he was unquestionably the new holder of the World's Bronc Riding title. Fellow aboriginal cowboys made a great commotion; whooping and chanting and ecstatically circling the ring on their horses.

Meanwhile Tom had to return to jail, although his confinement was sweetened by winning a medal, $1000 cash, a hand-made saddle and a champion belt with gold and silver mounted buckle.

This championship was to be Tom's chief claim to fame, although he was also an expert roper and continued to compete in rodeos in Calgary and elsewhere. He was a well-educated man, a promoter of progressive farming and ranching methods, and eventually he became quite wealthy. At his ranch near Spring Coulee, he bred racing thoroughbreds, owned a large herd of Hereford cattle and supplied bucking broncos for rodeos at Lethbridge, Raymond, Cardston and Taber.

An unfortunate accident occurred in 1946 when Tom tried to prevent a young colt from breaking out of a corral. Three Persons broke his pelvic bone on a rail and was permanently disabled. From then on his health declined and he died at Calgary's Holy Cross Hospital in 1949 at age 63.

His funeral at St. Mary's Catholic Church was attended by cowboys, First Nations, sportsmen and businessmen—the largest procession the Cardston church had ever witnessed. As reminders of his past glory, his photograph has a place of honour at the Blood Reserve community hall at Standoff, and his beaded buckskins are on display at the Fort Macleod Museum.

Stephan G. Stephansson

He was born in 1853 on a small farm on the north coast of Iceland. The farm was on rocky ground but Stephan's early life was rich. Although his formal education stopped at elementary school, the Icelandic custom of nightly family reading acquainted him with his country's abundant literary heritage. It didn't take Stephan long to contribute to that heritage. He began writing poetry at age 15 and his first book of poems was published by age 19. By his early 20s, he was hailed as the leading Icelandic poet in North America.

He had no money when he arrived in Alberta, and eked out a living by fishing, hunting and farming. Stephan also worked on a CPR survey crew to make ends meet. It wasn't a lucrative job: the surveyors were expected to pay for their room and board out of their $2.00 per day wages.

Despite his poverty, Stephan was active in the community. He was the first school board chairman of the Markerville School District and was one of the organizers of the Tindastoll Butter and Cheese Manufacturing Company. The new venture became the first source of steady income for the Icelandic settlers.

Stephan considered himself a Canadian, although he retained his affection for his homeland. He continued writing poetry whenever he found a moment, and much of his poetry reflects his love for Canada. The following passage is from his poem "Toast to Alberta":

"Here veils of Northern Light are drawn
On high as winter closes,
And hoary dews at summer dawn
Adorn the wild red roses.

Sometimes the swelling clouds of rain
Repress the sun's caresses;
But soon the mountains smile again
And shake their icy tresses."

His scholarly life set him apart from the other people in his community, and many of his opinions were unpopular among his contemporaries. He was deeply religious but was completely opposed to what he saw as the narrow-mindedness of the established churches.

In 1914 he became a bitter opponent of Canada's involvement in the First World War:

"In Europe's reeking slaughter-pen
They mince the flesh of murdered men,
While swinish merchants, snout in trough,
Drink all the bloody profits off!"

The other settlers in Markerville disapproved of Stephan for another reason as well. In their view, he was too fond of socializing and burdened his wife Helga with the responsibility of raising their five sons and three daughters. Stephan's fellow settlers may have misunderstood him, but they bought his books and were proud of his fame.

Following his death, they dedicated a community park to his memory and established the Stephan G. Stephansson Chapter of the Icelandic Society. His farmhouse still stands as a shrine for Icelandic people everywhere. It has since become an Alberta Historical Site. Throughout his life, Stephansson's fondest hope was to move people through his poetry:

"And when the last of all my days is over,
The last page turned,
And whatsoever shall be deemed in wages
That I have earned;
In such a mood I hope to be composing
My sweetest lay;
And then—extend my hand to all the world
And pass away."

Archibald Wayne Dingman

It started with the discovery of a well at Turner Valley and became the "Fantastic Calgary Oil Boom" of 1914. It was a spark that ignited nearly 400 new companies, emerging overnight in the expectation of big profits from oil. One oil historian later reported that "on Friday, every available motor vehicle in Calgary was forced into service, carrying hundreds of men to the foothills and the Dingman well."

The discovery well produced many other notable changes as well. Steel derricks replaced wooden ones. Twelve thousand producing wells and a bewildering array of special machines for production and distribution completely altered Alberta's pastoral landscape.

This extraordinary turn of events was set in motion by a man who once sold soap for a living. But he was born with a talent for business, and as a child growing up in Greenbush, Ontario in the late 1850s and 60s, Dingman educated himself on a variety of subjects that were to prove useful later on. He was one of nine children in a United Empire Loyalist family and as soon as he came of age, he headed for the developing Pennsylvania oil fields in the 1880s. It was there that he gained his first business experience in the oil industry. When he later returned to his homeland, his thoughts of searching for oil in Canada were discouraged for a variety of reasons, mainly financial. In the meantime, he became involved in a company that manufactured coaster brakes for bicycles. He also worked for the Scarborough Electric Railway, and his strong interest in electric lighting led him to become associated with the first company to install electric lights in Toronto and other cities. In fact, he was later to claim that he personally placed the first electric streetlight in Toronto.

His involvement with a soap company, which would have made him a millionaire, was cut short when the company burned to the ground in the great Toronto fire of 1900.

This calamity, along with his never-extinguished interest in searching for oil, led him to Calgary in 1902. There were numerous obstacles to overcome. The roads leading to what might prove to be an oil-bearing well were potholed and almost impassable. Field equipment was in pathetically short supply and had to be imported from the United States, frequently after long delays in shipping. The availability of geological data, let alone experienced wildcatters, was also severely limited. Furthermore, markets for gas and oil were almost completely undeveloped, meaning that the all-important dollar was a constant source of worry.

But Dingman persevered, and in 1905 he organized the Calgary Gas Company. His first well on the Sarcee Reserve proved unsuccessful although he optimistically declared a holiday thinking he had finally made it. The Walker Well, his company's second attempt, did contain gas in sufficient quantities to provide domestic fuel and

street lighting in East Calgary, after initially providing gas to the Calgary Brewing and Malting Company.

This success led him to pursue oil exploration in a big way, and he formed the Calgary Petroleum Products Company in 1912. It was this company that drilled the historic well in Turner Valley.

Dingman was a tireless worker and was hard at it until about two weeks prior to his death at 85. Even then, he had mapped out 20 years of future work in oil exploration. He also proved to be a prophet: his lifelong slogan was "Carry on, we want and need more crude oil."

James Bertram Collip

The discovery of insulin is popularly associated with the names Banting and Best. There were two other Canadians connected with the medical breakthrough in diabetes. One was Professor Macleod of the University of Toronto, and the other was an Albertan—James Bertram Collip.

Dr. Collip's contribution was to make insulin available for therapeutic use. He developed a technique using alcohol to remove toxic substances from it and to preserve it. Although he won the Nobel Prize for this work with Banting, Best and Macleod, he felt his share of the discovery "was only that which any well-trained biochemist would be expected to contribute." This modesty was characteristic.

He was above all a scientist, and a dedicated one. His early education was in a one-room country school in Belleville, Ontario, where he qualified to attend Trinity College at the University of Toronto by age 15. By the time he was 23, he had his PhD in biochemistry. In 1915, the University of Alberta offered him his first academic appointment as a lecturer in physiology and biochemistry.

He was a shy man and wasn't particularly comfortable standing in front of students. He also managed to pursue his personal research, often working through the night. His wife Ray, whom he had met at Trinity College, would often join him in the evenings.

In 1921, Dr. Collip received a Rockefeller Travelling Fellowship to go to Toronto to work on carbohydrate metabolism with Dr. Macleod. It was there that the fateful connection with Drs. Banting and Best occurred. He became fascinated with the new field of endocrinology, the study of glands that secrete hormones throughout the bloodstream.

Collip returned to the University of Alberta as Professor of Biochemistry in 1922, and decided to enter the Faculty of Medicine at the same time. He felt it would better equip him to understand the ways in which hormones affect the human body. He discovered a method of extracting a hormone from the parathyroid glands, and his finding provided relief for patients suffering from spasms of the voluntary muscles (parathyroid tetany). His methods soon became standard procedure in clinical laboratories throughout the world.

Although Collip had special fondness for Alberta (his three children were born in Edmonton), his particular brand of genius and integrity was in great demand. In 1928 he was invited to go to McGill University to head the Biochemistry Department. There he discovered that certain chemicals in the bloodstream affect people's personalities as well as their growth, their complexion and their energy level. Collip was also responsible for inventing a method of blood preservation, which was of great benefit in providing emergency relief for the wounded.

Collip received the Flavelle gold medal for distinguished work in the field of natural science as well as honorary degrees from virtually every university in Canada and a number in England and the United States. However, the friend who gave the eulogy at James Collip's funeral pointed out that a full life requires more than honorary bouquets. "We remember the intuitions which guided his experiments, the speed and fairness of his decisions and the velocity of his movements, his swiftness to praise and reluctance to blame, his timidity in his own defence and his fury in protection of his friends."

Emily Murphy

Born in 1868 in Cookstown, Ontario, Emily Ferguson graduated from the Bishop Strachan School in Toronto with a medal for general proficiency. While she was at school, she met a theology student named Arthur Murphy, whom she married at age 19. Arthur's outstanding ability as a preacher soon led to a position in London with a British missionary society. Emily found herself having to defend Canadians to the rather disdainful British, and earned herself the nickname "Janey Canuck." Later she adopted this moniker as her pen-name when the couple returned to Canada and her writing career started to flourish.

They moved to Swan Lake, Manitoba. There she wrote book reviews for the *Winnipeg Telegram*, and her collection of articles on pioneer life called *Janey Canuck in the West* became a best-seller. At the same time, she was responsible for managing their 320-acre farm while Arthur was occupied in the timber business.

When the Murphys moved to Edmonton in 1907, her interests became increasingly political. It seemed that she succeeded at whatever she took on. One important victory was the passage of The Dower Act, a piece of legislation that gave women a share in their husbands' homesteads. Her demands for a court that dealt exclusively with women's problems were also successful. Emily Murphy was appointed magistrate; she seemed stern and forbidding in her office, but her fundamental viewpoint was that lawbreakers should be rehabilitated rather than punished.

One lawyer, Eardly Jackson, refused to accept her judgements because she was not legally a "person." Other lawyers followed suit, but the Alberta Supreme Court upheld her authority. Still, at the federal level, women could not be admitted to the Senate because the British North America Act did not recognize them as "persons." Emily became embroiled in a battle that "took me thirteen years and almost broke my heart." Despite a vigorous press campaign, and the support of Canadian women's groups, the federal government did nothing to change the situation. Eventually Emily initiated an

appeal to the Supreme Court of
Canada, along with four other
women—Nellie McClung, Irene
Parlby, Henrietta Edwards and
Louise McKinney. This appeal
also failed. The last resort was
the Privy Council of England.
Finally, in 1929, that court
decreed that women were indeed
persons.

Ironically, the success of this
judgement contained within it
the greatest disappointment of
Emily's career. Emily was an
obvious choice for senator, but
was overlooked for a variety of
reasons. One senator explained,
"Oh, we never could have had
Mrs. Murphy in the Senate! She
would have caused too much
trouble."

She did indeed cause trouble—exposing the evils of the narcotics
trade in a world-renowned book called *The Black Candle*. She also
promoted birth control at a time when such a thing was unheard of.

Immediately before her death in 1933, she visited the court where
she had served for 17 years. On that occasion someone said of her,
"We are honoured today by the presence of Mrs. Emily Murphy,
Police Magistrate and Judge. A feminine note missing from this
building...is brought back by the kindly, smiling countenance of this
beloved lady." The speaker was none other than Eardly Jackson, the
lawyer who had repeatedly challenged her authority years before.

William Pearce

The career of William Pearce, "Czar of the Prairies" and "Father of Southern Alberta Irrigation," spanned an era of high adventure, dramatic change and big ideas. Born in 1848 in Elgin County, Ontario, he started his government duties as a land surveyor. For him, that meant travelling to the unsettled West by dog team, sleeping under sled dogs for warmth and living on wild meat, hard tack, pemmican and tea. He was a big man, well suited to this rugged life. Once when he fell into a frozen river, narrowly escaping drowning, he discovered that the layer of ice on top of his clothing provided good insulation against the cold. He tried to persuade the other men in his party to do the same. They were not interested.

In over 30 years as a land surveyor throughout the then North-West Territories, Pearce became very familiar with both the issues and the resources of western Canada, prior to the creation of the new province. Pearce was responsible for attracting the attention of the Dominion government to the need for irrigation in what is now southern Alberta. At first the government was not receptive to his

ideas. Potential settlers might be discouraged if the government itself admitted that water was in short supply. Nonetheless, Pearce persevered.

Once, when he was making a presentation to the government, Members of Parliament claimed to be ignorant of exactly what irrigation was. The exasperated Pearce suggested taking a look at the lawn sprinklers on the Parliament grounds might help clarify things for them.

Back home in Calgary, he made a public example of the benefits of irrigation by piping water from Bragg Creek onto his land. His neighbours were astounded by the quality and quantity of grains and vegetables this produced.

Severe drought in southern Alberta in the 1890s strengthened Pearce's case, and his efforts were eventually rewarded with the passage of The Northwest Irrigation Act in 1894. A number of the irrigation projects promoted by Pearce were ahead of their time. One of these projects was the Bassano Dam, which he proposed because the CPR was having problems getting enough water to run its locomotives in the southern part of the province. As Pearce phrased it, "We could get water from the eastern area for locomotives, for irrigation and for stock watering purposes. We could change the face of the country."

Pearce claimed that by taking water from the North Saskatchewan, Clearwater and Red Deer rivers and storing it in Sullivan Lake, over a million acres in central Alberta and west-central Saskatchewan could be irrigated. He was convinced the idea was completely practical. It terrified government officials of his time, and it is still controversial today.

Pearce was also outspoken about the conservation of natural resources—an idea that few of his contemporaries understood. William Van Horne, president of the CPR and a personal friend of Pearce's, was an exception. When Pearce was a member of the Dominion Lands Board, Van Horne encouraged him to reserve 26 square kilometres around the Banff Hot Springs as government land. This small beginning opened the door to Canada's system of national parks.

William Pearce was a man of great schemes and grandiose imaginings. His sandstone mansion in East Calgary had 15 rooms and 3 fireplaces. It was affectionately referred to by Calgarians as the "Bow Bend Shack." Pearce would have been disappointed to know that it was torn down in 1957. Alberta's parks and irrigation programs and resource development reflect much more effectively his concern for the needs of future generations.

William Griesbach

William Antrobus Griesbach was born to be a soldier. His father, equally military, had been the first man to join the North-West Mounted Police.

The future Canadian general was born at Fort Qu'Appelle, in what is now Saskatchewan, in 1878. In 1899, he served with the Canadian Mounted Rifles in the South African War. He was a slight man, weighing only 138 pounds, but he used his ingenuity to attain the 140-pound military requirement by concealing a two-pound lump of coal behind his back while being weighed. He also astounded the military doctors with what they thought was his extraordinary eyesight. William had committed to memory the calendar they used in the examination, including the fine print. Enroute overseas, he passed through Regina and there approached the Benchers of the Law Society of the Territories to permit him a pass for his final examination in law. Although he had not read all of the prescribed books, he managed to confound the Benchers with a discussion on wills that lasted the entire examination period. He was thereby admitted to the bar at age 22 and later became the senior member of the law firm of Griesbach and O'Connor.

When he returned from South Africa, he became an alderman in Edmonton in 1905. Two years later, at the age of 29, he was elected mayor. Griesbach felt that city council members should be paid businessmen's salaries. This opinion was not particularly popular with voters, but bowing to the views of others was not a concern of Griesbach's.

On two occasions, in 1905 and 1913, he attempted to get elected as a Conservative member of the provincial legislature, and was defeated both times. His attempt to get elected to the federal House of Commons in 1911 was equally unsuccessful.

On the outbreak of the Great War in 1914, he volunteered for service in the Canadian Expeditionary Force and quickly distinguished himself. He led the 49th Battalion in active duty in France.

Soldiers of the battalion remember him as hard, but very just, never forcing them into battlefield conditions he was unwilling to risk himself. For his outstanding military service he was decorated with the Distinguished Service Order (DSO) and bar.

After returning from overseas, he ran against Liberal incumbent Frank Oliver in the 1917 federal election. His opponent bitterly commented on Griesbach's candidacy in *The Bulletin*: "That Col. Griesbach returned from England to Canada in the supposed interests of the Conservative Party rather than in the interests of the Empire is made amply evident by the acceptance of the party nomination for West Edmonton... Clearly...he was thought to be a party necessity if there was to be a hope of carrying the constituency for the government."

It did nothing to halt Griesbach's political career. In 1921, at the age of 44, Prime Minister Arthur Meighen appointed him to the Senate. Twenty years later he became Inspector General of Western Canadian Forces.

In the years prior to his death in 1945, he wrote his autobiography, entitled *I Remember*. The book shows an entirely different side to "Billy" Griesbach. He reveals himself as a rare and witty man, with the ability to laugh at his own mistakes.

1919–

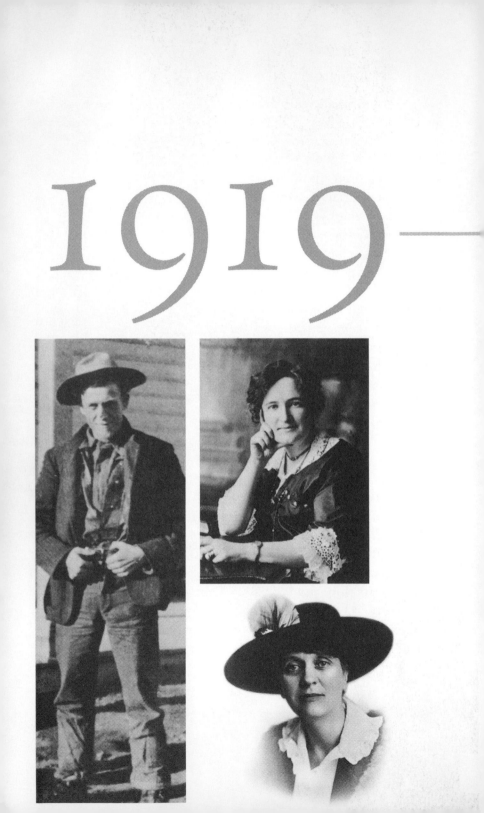

1929

A New Furrow...

Young farm boys returned from the Great War in Europe (1914–18) impatient with the old order and bewildered by change that had already come to Alberta.

Inflation, unemployment, Prohibition and bitter political wars greeted the returning soldiers.

The grim tensions eased with prosperity and significant political change.

Henry Wise Wood

He was acclaimed "the Uncrowned King of Alberta" and "the Moses of Alberta Farmers." Henry's father had served in the Confederate army and was a prosperous farmer in Missouri, where Henry was born in 1860. In the fashion of that place and time, his father was also a slave-owner, although Henry remembered the slaves as being treated more like members of the family.

Henry Wise Wood's earliest ambition was to enter the ministry. But in the 1890s, he became involved in the Farmers' Equity Movement, an organization dedicated to promoting the rights of farmers. His own farming operations in both Missouri and Texas were very successful. However, at the age of 45, he saw Alberta as an opportunity to fulfill his boyhood dream of becoming a cowboy. Alberta had just become a province and, to him, it was the "finest in the world."

Henry Wise Wood maintained there was "no use holding a membership of citizenship unless one is going to use it." In 1909, he joined the United Farmers of Alberta (UFA), and in 1911, he took out his Canadian citizenship. In both cases, his commitment was whole hearted.

At the time, Alberta farmers had had to accept what the buyer was willing to pay for their products. Henry's answer was "Organize! You will never get anything in this world that you do not get for yourself." Through Henry's efforts, Alberta farmers gained a sense of their own value. As a result, some 30,000 Alberta farmers became united; they were a force to be reckoned with, both provincially and federally.

Wise Wood was also a pivotal figure in the creation of wheat pools in Alberta. "If the government will not provide a wheat board, the farmers...can create their own." Wheat pools gave farmers control over the marketing of their grain and thanks to Wise Wood, the Alberta Wheat Pool was formed in 1923. He also helped farmers in Saskatchewan and Manitoba establish their own wheat pools. Wise Wood had a vision of farmers from Argentina, Australia and the United States uniting with Canadian farmers in a common purpose.

Wise Wood was opposed to the UFA becoming a political party, feeling it would undermine the organization's grass-roots strength. Other members disagreed and urged that the UFA run candidates in the 1921 election. Henry bowed to the will of the majority and dropped everything to work on the campaign. The UFA formed the government and Wise Wood seemed the logical choice for premier. But he declined political office, although many considered him the most influential man in Alberta throughout the 1920s. He died in Calgary in 1941.

Fred Brewster

Frederick Archibald Brewster lived in the Rockies for nearly 70 years. The title "Gentleman of the Mountains" was well deserved. The mountains were his lifeblood, his greatest passion. Brewster came by his attachment honestly. His father John once said, "Most people are hemmed in by clocks and timetables and their molehills become mountains. The first time they see a mountain they put the molehill in its proper place." In 1887, when Fred was three years old, the Brewsters moved to Banff. The family was to figure prominently in such tourist enterprises as Banff's Mount Royal Hotel, the Kananaskis Dude Ranch and the Brewster Transport Company.

Fred had to leave the mountains to complete his high school education at St. John's College in Winnipeg and to obtain a mining engineering degree at Queen's University in Kingston. But he could not leave them behind forever, and he soon made his home in Jasper. When he was 20 years old, he and a companion spent a full year

packing and canoeing through the
Cariboo country. He wintered at
Finlay River under conditions that
might discourage the average mor-
tal. In Fred's mind, "the stars always
shone brightly and seemed very
near in the mountain air. Other-
wise we were alone in a mighty
world of peaks, glaciers and snow."

His knowledge of the mountains was sought out by such
organizations as the Smithsonian

Institute and the United States Department of Biological Survey.
He led explorers and hunting parties, tracking down ranges of big
game and researching and collecting specimens north of the
Yellowhead Pass. On one of these trips, Brewster and his party
established the northern boundary of the Rocky Mountain Big
Sheep range. On another journey, he discovered the dominant
mountain west of Grande Prairie. He named it Mount Sir
Alexander, after the first white man to travel through the Rockies. It
was a personal crusade of Brewster that tribute should be paid to fur
trade explorers like Thompson, Fraser and others who risked their
lives exploring new lands. In turn, he noted that Jasper House,
Howse Pass, Jasper Lake, Jasper Park Lodge and Jasper National
Park were named after an obscure fur trade bookkeeper named
Jasper Howse. Brewster was irked that the First Nations name for
Jasper National Park, "The Land of Glittering Mountains" was
replaced by a white man's name.

Fred returned from one of his back-country trips to discover that
a war was underway in Europe. He immediately joined the 2nd
Tunneling Division of the Canadian Engineers. He rose swiftly to
the rank of major and in 1917 was decorated with the Military
Cross and Bar.

After the war he returned to Jasper and set about making the
mountains more accessible to visitors. He helped blaze new trails for

horseback trips, including the Skyline Trail to Maligne Lake. Fred Brewster guided thousands of visitors from across Canada, the United States and Europe on big game hunts, trail rides and long hikes through the back country by ski and snowshoe.

He remained a cross-country skier and vigorous walker until very late in life and lived to the age of 85. Appropriately, he was buried in the cemetery in Jasper, surrounded by his beloved mountains: "There seems no end to this vast, white land. But it is not a dead land. It is very much alive —alive with veins of fire that glint in the sun."

Irene Parlby

When Mary Irene Marry at first came to Alberta, she was fresh from a background that included a Continental education and a life of ease among the aristocracy of England and British India. Even though she had to learn such tasks as cooking, cleaning, washing and ironing from scratch, she was captivated by the quiet, open spaces and the fellowship among the scattered souls in her community. Besides, she saw life in Alix as an opportunity to make her own way. She had met and married Walter Parlby, a graduate of Oxford who shared her love of gardening, literature and theatre. The new English bride caused some talk in Alix ,with her fondness for pretty clothes, bronco riding, fine china and buckskins.

She was well aware that the lives of her neighbours were much less stimulating than her own. She became involved in setting up a women's group for mutual help and education. The community group evolved into the Women's Auxiliary of the United Farmers of Alberta, a province-wide organization.

Irene felt "farm women realize there are other things of interest in the world, and that they do their housekeeping all the better for thinking of outside affairs." These turned out to be prophetic words that hurled Irene into the political arena. The United Farmers of

Alberta were transforming from an economic pressure group into a political party. Irene was asked to run for office in the Lacombe riding in the 1921 election. She won, and the UFA formed the government.

The experience was an eye-opener. "I never realized until my first campaign in 1921 what miserable, incompetent creatures women were in the eyes of the public. I ought to have developed a terrible inferiority complex by the time it was over, for practically the only issue that seemed to concern the electorate or the opposition, was that I was a woman and worse, an English woman."

Irene was concerned with other issues. Her persuasiveness, humanitarian ideals and good judgement earned her the respect of her male colleagues. She was appointed Minister Without Portfolio in Premier Herbert Greenfield's Cabinet, only the second woman in the British Empire to achieve such an appointment.

While her portfolio was officially unnamed, her responsibilities were very clear in her own mind. She fought to improve laws affecting the lives of women and children. These efforts included legislation to provide municipal hospitals, public health nurses, child welfare clinics, minimum wages for women, property rights for married women and immigration laws to prevent settlers from being exploited. She was also a member of the "Famous Five" who gave Canadian women the right to be officially considered "persons" and eligible as members of the Canadian Senate.

Her greatest interest was "education, education and more education," and she was involved in projects to upgrade the schooling of all children. Her dedication led to an honorary Doctor of Laws degree from the University of Alberta, another first for Canadian women.

Despite her successes, Irene Parlby found much of the talk and paperwork associated with political office boring and disillusioning. She once confessed that, having left public life, she was strongly tempted to throw all the political documents and papers into a huge bonfire and dance around it.

After the exhausting 1930 election campaign (another aspect of public life she considered a waste of time), she was asked by Prime Minister Bennett to represent Canada at a League of Nations meeting in Geneva. Her Alberta supporters persuaded her to continue in office until the end of her term in 1935.

In private life, her services as a public speaker and writer continued to be in great demand, and she pursued these interests until her death in 1969 at the age of 97. Her leadership in fighting for women's rights, education and improvement of welfare benefits links her with a proud tradition of Alberta women pioneers.

Nellie McClung

Some called her "Windy Nellie," "Calamity Nell," "Holy Terror" and "The Hyena in Petticoats." The Manitoba Conservatives once burned her in effigy.

The real Nellie Letitia Mooney McClung was a warm-hearted, humorous woman. She was the youngest of six children in an Irish farm family in Ontario in 1873. The Mooneys moved to Wawanesa, Manitoba, when Nellie was six years old. At that time the tiny community had no school, which meant that she didn't learn to read until she was 10 years old. However, her ability as a student proved outstanding, and she became a qualified teacher and novice writer by the time she was 16.

From a very early age she challenged the inequality between the sexes. She found an ally in Wes McClung, the son of a minister.

After her marriage to him, her mother-in-law encouraged Nellie to pursue her writing, which led to publication of her first novel, *Sowing Seeds in Danny*. Her mentor encouraged Nellie to read sections of the book at meetings of the Women's Christian Temperance Union (WCTU), which gave the young bride her first invaluable experience in public speaking.

Nellie became involved in the Winnipeg Political Equality League, an organization dedicated to securing the vote for women. When conventional methods failed, drastic measures were in order. The result was a Women's Mock Parliament, staged at Winnipeg's Walker Theatre. In the play, men were put in the position of being denied the vote. Nellie's speech brought down the house in gales of laughter: "The trouble is that if men start to vote, they will vote too much. Politics unsettles men, and unsettled men means unsettled bills, broken furniture, broken vows and divorce. If men were to get into the habit of voting, who knows what might happen—it's hard enough to keep them at home now."

The play was successful and so was the argument. In 1916, Manitoba women received the vote.

Nellie's activities in the suffrage movement carried her throughout North America. Neighbours hinted darkly that she neglected her children and that her marriage was hovering near divorce. It was far from true. Her marriage was a happy one and her husband applauded her activities. As a joke, he trained their son to respond to anti-suffragists with the line, "My name is Mark McClung. My mother is a suffragist, and I have never known a mother's love."

In 1921, shortly after the family moved to Alberta, Nellie was elected to the legislature as a Liberal member of the Opposition. Irene Parlby sat on the opposite side of the house as a member of the United Farmers of Alberta party. Together they supported social welfare causes such as public health nurses, municipal hospitals, liberalized property laws for women and improved health and education for school children. Both joined with Emily Murphy in the famous "Persons Case" to give women the official right as "persons" to become members of the Canadian Senate.

She never backed down from anything she believed in—"Never retract, never explain, never apologize; get the thing done and let them howl!" She handled her political defeat in 1926 by embarking on a "baking binge," and then got on with her family life and her writing.

Nellie McClung was the first Canadian, male or female, to make a living as an author. Prior to her death in Victoria in 1951 at age 68, she had published 16 books, as well as innumerable magazine and newspaper articles. Her eloquent arguments in favour of women's liberation, in fact human liberation, could easily have been written today:

"The time will come, we hope, when women will be economically free, and mentally and spiritually independent enough to refuse to have their food paid for by men, when women will receive equal pay for equal work, and have all avenues of activity open to them; and will be free to choose their own mates, without shame, or indelicacy; when men will not be afraid of marriage because of the financial burden, but free men and free women will marry for love, and together work for the sustenance of their families."

Karl Clark

Peter Pond, the first trader to travel down the Athabasca River, was impressed by the tar sands and remarked on them in his diaries. About these same Athabasca tar sands, Karl Adolf Clark said, "They have been a taunt to North America for generations. They wear a smirk which seems to say: When are you going to do something?" He spent his lifetime answering their challenge.

Clark was born in 1888 in Georgetown, Ontario. He got his first opportunity to "do something" in 1920, when Dr. Henry Marshall Tory invited him to join the newly formed Research Council of Alberta. He was asked to head the Road Materials Section, which involved developing a method to use the oil sands for paving roads. It was a pioneering effort for which Clark was well qualified: he had been Chief Road Materials Engineer for the Canadian government.

When Clark arrived in Edmonton, he began the research that was to affect tar sands extraction all over the world. The technique he evolved is known as the "water flotation extraction method." It involved mixing strip-mined, oil-bearing sand with hot water and then skimming off the bitumen tar when it rose to the surface. The tar was put through further extraction and refining processes to obtain a usable product called "synthetic crude."

When World War II broke out and large amounts of oil were needed to meet war-time needs, Dr. Clark began researching other aspects of petroleum extraction. The government financed the construction of an extraction plant at Bitmount on the Athabasca River. Dr. Clark's hot-water process proved very successful. Major oil companies became interested in the Athabasca oil sands. Great Canadian Oil Sands (GCOS) decided to act, and Dr. Clark became central to their operation. He soon became an international advisor to industry and government.

Despite his achievements, Dr. Clark remained a modest man who gave equal credit to those who had helped him with his work. He retained his office at the Research Council (taking his cocker spaniel with him to work every day) and continued finding solutions to oil sands problems.

For a man who had committed three decades of his life to oil sands research, the greatest reward would have been to see the GCOS plant go into operation. It occurred in 1967, a year after his death.

J. Percy Page

Most people, when they think about the years they spent in school, can remember at least one teacher who set what seemed impossibly high standards. J. Percy Page, who taught commercial education in the Edmonton school system for 40 years, was that kind of teacher. And he got results.

Born in Rochester, New York in 1887 to Canadian parents, John Percy Page was also a fantastic basketball coach. In 1914 a group of girls at his Edmonton school asked him if he would coach their team. He said he would give it a try and began drilling his players in shooting and passing during two weekly 90-minute practice sessions. By the end of their first year, the Commercial Grads walked off with the City Championship.

From then on, there was no looking back. Page inspired clean, simple plays, and the "Grads," over a period of 25 years, won 502 out of 522 games. They travelled the globe, played at four Olympic meets and held the world title for 17 consecutive years.

But once World War II began, the fifth Olympic games were cancelled. Also, the Grads' arena, the Edmonton Gardens, was taken over by the British Commonwealth Air Training force. 1940 was the final year for the Grads— the team with the greatest record in sports history. As for Percy Page, he went on to become principal of the commercial section at Victoria Composite High School. When he retired in 1952, he was quoted as "wondering what I'll do with my time." The answer came four days later when he became house leader for the Alberta Progressive Conservative Party. It wasn't his first foray into politics. He had long been active in citizens' associations and had sat in the legislature as an independent member. Throughout his political life he lobbied for reforms that favoured "the little guy": reducing federal taxes, making the provincial government responsible for health and social assistance programs. He felt the Social Credit party policy of subsidizing oil companies was not benefiting the people of Alberta. He also accused the Manning government of "railroading" pupils through Alberta high schools, claiming the system was "not producing the educated men and women the province needed."

Page was defeated in the 1959 provincial election, but shortly thereafter Prime Minister John Diefenbaker appointed him lieutenant-governor of Alberta. In 1964, Prime Minister Lester Pearson extended his term. He continued in that office until his retirement in 1966. At the time of Page's death at age 85 in 1973, a close friend described him as a man "standing on tiptoe...the better to discover what life is really all about."

Roland Gissing

The beauty of Alberta's scenery—its mountains, its foothills and its prairies—is now famous worldwide. Much of the credit for this acclaim must go to an artist named Roland Gissing, whose paintings hang in galleries throughout North America and Europe. Reproductions of his work also adorn calendars, Christmas cards and books around the world.

Gissing came to Alberta from his native England in 1913, when he was just 16 years old. He had seen American movies of the Wild West, and his greatest dream was to be a cowboy. At first, he had to settle for a job looking after ponies for a polo club near Calgary. But he bought a pair of cowboy chaps with his first pay cheque, and managed to get hired on as a cowhand at a ranch near Crossfield. He continued riding the range for the next 10 years, sketching ranch scenes along the way. It wasn't until he settled near Cochrane in the mid-1920s that he began taking his painting seriously. He educated himself by studying great masters. In 1929, this work culminated in a very successful one-man show at an art gallery in Calgary. However, with the arrival of the Great Depression, Gissing's plans to open his own studio met with financial disaster. He was forced to get work decorating the walls of the Hudson's Bay Cafeteria and the Club Cafe.

He soon returned to Cochrane, got married and resumed his painting. He spent his summer days sketching, going into the mountains for weeks at a time. During the winter he painted, usually in oils. Gissing also developed a passion for model railways, which he made entirely by hand. The engines actually worked, and one locomotive could pull more than a ton!

In 1944 his home and studio, which he had largely built himself, were completely destroyed by fire. He felt the loss of his model railway even more keenly than the destruction of his books and paintings. However, he picked up the pieces, rebuilt a new home and studio, and carried on.

Unlike most artists, Gissing was recognized by the international art community during his lifetime. By the time he reached middle age, art connoisseurs were eager to obtain "early Gissings" for their private collections. One early work, an enormous painting of a buffalo hunt, once decorated the outside wall of a service station in Banff!

The artist himself was a quiet, modest man who used his painting to help him come to terms with his greatest love, nature. Although the Rocky Mountains intimidated him, he always portrayed them as restful. His landscapes speak a language that everyone can understand and enjoy, and his work has brought delight to thousands of people throughout the world.

Herman Trelle

The Peace River district wasn't always considered a fertile agricultural belt. But Herman Trelle once boasted it could grow everything except grapefruit. And he almost proved it. Along the way, he also picked up some 135 championships for various crops including wheat, oats and field peas. He put the Peace River Country onto the world agricultural map.

He was educated in Edmonton and on family trips to Germany. His first championship wasn't in agriculture, but in public speaking when, at

17, he became Edmonton's top boy orator. The First World War cut short his engineering studies at the University of Alberta. To his bitter disappointment, his German-American background disqualified him from military service, so he followed his parents to Peace River and began farming.

In 1918, he made another attempt to enlist, this one successful. He joined the Royal Flying Corps, but the war ended soon after. Back on the farm he began experimenting with cross-breeding strains of wheat. He concentrated on varieties of Marquis wheat, which had proven so successful on the Canadian prairies. By 1920 he was growing his own registered grain, and six years later he captured the world wheat championship in Chicago. The same year, his Victory oats took the world honours.

Herman Trelle continued his experiments, branching out into hybrid projects involving flowers, vegetables and fruit. In 1928, the Alberta government set aside a farm near Wembley for his various testing programs. Poor health kept him away from the world wheat championships in 1929, but he made up for it by winning the award in each of the next three years.

In 1932, he was barred from contesting the world wheat title for three years because he had won it too often. As soon as he became eligible again, in 1936, he was once more named top world wheat grower.

Although Trelle complained that he didn't make much money as a championship grower, he certainly earned an international reputation. He was not modest about any of his achievements, either. He once bragged to the dean of the University of Alberta agricultural school that he could talk in 10 languages. "You know, Herman," the dean replied, "you should learn to keep quiet in 10 languages."

In World War II, he enlisted with the Royal Canadian Engineers and served briefly in Ontario before being discharged for medical reasons. The overseas duty he wanted eluded him for good.

Herman Trelle never returned to farming. After two years as a munitions inspector with the CPR in Calgary, he moved to California. A few months later, as supervisor of ranch holdings for the Overholtz Company, the world-famed grower met a tragic death: he was shot and fatally wounded by a ranch-hand whom he had fired the day before.

Jimmy Simpson

Of all the so-called "mountain men" of Alberta, perhaps the best-known was Justin James McCartney Simpson. But when a mountain was named after him in 1974, it became just plain Mount Jimmy Simpson.

He came to Alberta from England in 1896 when he was 18, at a time when no superhighways cut through the rugged Rocky Mountains. A CPR conductor found him sleeping aboard his train with no ticket, and put him off at Lake Louise. Jimmy promptly got a job as a railway section hand. Later he went to the West Coast and signed on with a seal-hunting crew. One morning, he overslept and missed his boat. The Russians arrested the crew and sentenced the men to exile in Siberia; Jimmy missed out on that too. He also missed a prison term when he turned down an invitation to join the train-robbing gang led by Bill Miner.

Jimmy Simpson returned to the mountains and stayed there for over 70 years. He became one of the most popular guides in the area. He called his clients "pilgrims." They included such people as American humourist Will Rogers, singer-actor Burl Ives, novelist Jack London and hockey commentator Foster Hewitt. "Some of them took to the wilds like fish take to water," he said. "Others should have stayed home."

One of Jimmy Simpson's main concerns was the precious water resources of the mountain glaciers. He predicted that Albertans could be forced to buy drinking water by the bottle in the next century if they didn't preserve it now. "The ordinary person is not paying enough attention to tomorrow," he complained.

Another concern was the "softness" of modern life. "People don't want to go anywhere today unless there's a good road and they can take their car."

Jimmy Simpson wasn't soft. He once hiked 120 kilometres by snowshoe to spend Christmas with his friend Tom Wilson, the famous guide who had discovered Lake Louise. The next day he turned around and hiked back. On the way he cheated death three times. The first was when he broke through the ice of the North Saskatchewan River. Then he was caught in a small avalanche. Later, at his camp, he realized just in time that the white powder dropping into his frying pan wasn't snow. It was strychnine poison, which he carried to bait fox traps.

In the 1920s, Jimmy Simpson built a lodge called Num-Ti-Jah at Bow Lake, north of Lake Louise. Thousands of summer visitors came to appreciate this small, wiry "mountain man" with his glacier-blue eyes, his storyteller's wit and his ever-present Mountie-style hat.

The Stoney called Jimmy Simpson Nashan-esen because of his speed on snowshoes. The name means "wolverine-go-quick."

Until his death in 1972, Simpson maintained a keen interest in literature and opera. He could speak with anyone on almost any topic. At 83 he took up the hobby of watercolour painting. Above all, though, Jimmy Simpson was a man of the mountains who respected the lesson of the outdoors: "If you listen, the wilderness teaches you. If you don't, it can kill you."

W.R. "Wop" May

The bush pilots who opened up Canada's North were pioneers, daredevils and, in a sense, nation-builders. They really were "magnificent men in their flying machines." Among the greatest was "Wop" May. He was also "one of the finest natural flyers in the history of aviation."

Wilfred Reid May was born in 1896 in Carberry, Manitoba, but came to Edmonton at the age of six. When he died 50 years later he left a remarkable string of accomplishments behind him.

As a young pilot in the First World War, he made his first combat flight on April 21, 1918 in a Sopwith Camel. That flight made history. He was chased by Baron Manfred Von Richtofen, the German ace known as the "Red Baron." May's guns jammed, but he outmanoeuvred Richtofen for miles. Finally the German plane was shot down by another Canadian, Captain Roy Brown, a former schoolmate of Wop May's in Edmonton. May returned from the war with less than a year of combat experience. Yet he was given credit for shooting down 13 enemy planes and received the Distinguished Flying Cross.

Commercial aviation was still in its infancy when he got back to Canada. His pilot's licence was only the seventh issued in Canada. He and his brother, Court, formed Edmonton's first air service. Their plane, the "City of Edmonton," was a Curtiss Jenny owned by the city. For some time Wop May made his living "barnstorming" — taking curious passengers on short flights for a fee. To the thrill of first flight was added the honour of riding with a genuine war ace.

Pilots of the 1920s were often their own mechanics, especially on flights to remote areas. Once, after being stranded near Whitecourt, May used bacon rind and friction tape to repair a leaky radiator hose.

The year 1929 began with a mercy flight to Fort Vermilion. The community was threatened by a diphtheria epidemic. May and his co-pilot, Vic Horner, set out on the 800-kilometre flight to deliver the needed antitoxin on January 3. Their plane had open cockpits and was equipped with wheels rather than skis. The temperature was well below zero. To keep the antitoxin from freezing they used charcoal burners during the flight. The mission was a success. Severely wind-chilled, the two men returned to Edmonton as heroes.

Later that year May became the first person to fly to the Arctic Ocean in winter. That air mail flight to Aklavik was one of many pioneering mail runs into the Far North. In 1930, Wop received the McKee Trophy for "the most meritorious service for the advancement of Canadian aviation."

In 1932, he had a ringside seat for another drama that made headlines around the world. He assisted the RCMP in their search for Albert Johnson, the "Mad Trapper of Rat River." May was there when the chase across the Arctic ended in the deranged killer's death on February 17. It was the first time an aircraft had been used in a Canadian manhunt.

Wop May was made an Officer of the Order of the British Empire in 1935. That honour was chiefly for the 1929 mercy flight—just one of his pioneering experiences.

In World War II, May served as supervisor of training for Canadian pilots. His development of a "search and rescue" service for airmen earned him the "Bronze Pal"—the American Medal of Freedom given by the U.S. government. He died in 1952.

When he was inducted into the Canadian Aviation Hall of Fame in 1973, he was remembered for his "aeronautical brilliance in the crudest geographic arenas, [and] his total dedication to the cause of uniting people through air transport…"

Even Baron Von Richtofen would have admired him.

Louise McKinney

Just one year after Alberta women gained the right to vote in 1916, Roberta MacAdam and Louise McKinney became the first women ever elected to a legislature in the British Empire. The first to take office was Louise McKinney.

She was born Louise Crummy in Frankville, Ontario, one of 10 children of Irish immigrants. Although she described herself as a "home woman" whose public activities in the temperance movement, politics and church work remained secondary to her family commitments, Louise McKinney was an outspoken supporter of women's rights. "Even as a child," she said, "I recognized and resented the disabilities laid upon women."

She had wanted to become a doctor, but instead settled for the life of a schoolteacher. While teaching in North Dakota, she met James McKinney, who shared her deep concern about the harmful effects of alcohol and tobacco. They were married in 1896 and moved to Claresholm, seven years later.

In 1917, Louise McKinney was elected to the Alberta legislature as a candidate for the Non-Partisan League. As a new MLA, Louise McKinney was the object of much scorn when she tried to prevent tobacco rations from being sent to Canadian troops fighting in Europe. She also supported aid for immigrants and the mentally disabled, and for widows and deserted wives. She spoke out for strict enforcement of liquor control laws. With Henrietta Muir Edwards, she drafted a Dower Act, which guaranteed Alberta widows a part of their husbands' estates.

After four years in office she was defeated by 45 votes when the United Farmers of Alberta swept into power. Louise McKinney made her mark as a church worker. In 1925 she became the only woman to sign the "Basis of Union," which created the United Church of Canada.

Perhaps the high point of Louise McKinney's public career came in 1928, when she was one of five women to petition Ottawa for a ruling on the question of women being qualified to sit in the Canadian Senate. It became known as the "Persons Case." The Supreme Court of Canada ruled that, under the British North America Act, women were not "eligible persons" for Senate appointment. A year later the British Privy Council overturned that decision in one of the most important legal rulings in Canadian history.

She never gave up her battle against tobacco and alcohol. For more than 20 years she was both Alberta president and Dominion vice-president of the Women's Christian Temperance Union. She died in 1931.

1930–

1938

The Lean Years...

A decade of prosperity and social innovation
left Albertans unprepared
for the lean years that followed.

Drought at home and a worldwide
economic depression drove the province
into new political directions.

The Great Depression was to shape
the mentality of a generation and
leave an enduring scar on the
political memory of a province.

R.B. Bennett

Two Canadian prime ministers have come from Alberta. Both were Conservatives, but that is where the resemblance ends. The first was Richard Bedford Bennett, a wealthy, aristocratic, bachelor lawyer. He was born in 1870 in Hopewell Cape, New Brunswick and died in 1947 in Mickleham, England. Although he represented Calgary in the House of Commons for two decades, he "never really became a westerner," according to one biographer.

Before entering law school, he taught school in New Brunswick. By the time he was 18, he had been principal of four schools with 140 students—for $500 a year! Before he was 20, Bennett declared that he would be prime minister one day. His involvement in politics

began when he ran successfully as an alderman in Chatham, New Brunswick. His campaign had been run by a lifelong friend, Max Aitken, who later became Lord Beaverbrook.

R.B. Bennett came to Calgary in 1897 as law partner of Senator James Lougheed. His association with Senator Lougheed made him a rich man. His own drive and ability earned him widespread respect as a corporate lawyer in both Canada and England.

After less than two years in the West he won a seat in the Territorial Assembly. He lost by only 29 votes when he ran for Alberta's first provincial legislature in 1905. In 1909, he was successful, but he stayed in provincial politics for only two years before going to the House of Commons. In 1914, he opposed his party leader, Robert Borden, over a railway agreement, so he did not contest the 1917 election.

Between 1917 and 1925, he was often in England arguing cases before the British Privy Council. The Lougheed-Bennett partnership fell apart during this period, and R.B. Bennett made his second fortune when he inherited the pulp and paper empire of a childhood friend, Jennie Shirreff Eddy.

He returned to Parliament in 1925 and served as Minister of Justice in Arthur Meighen's three-month government of 1926. The following year he succeeded Meighen as Conservative leader. In 1930, with the Great Depression underway, his party swept William Lyon Mackenzie King's Liberals out of office with a promise to "blast a way into the markets of the world." Five years later Mackenzie King, also a wealthy bachelor, swept back in with the slogan "King or Chaos."

One achievement of the Bennett era that survives is the Canadian Broadcasting Corporation. In its last months, his government also introduced several measures to tackle Depression problems. These included unemployment insurance, farm credit, minimum wage laws, agricultural marketing boards and restrictions on unfair trade practices (later declared unconstitutional).

R.B. Bennett's own efforts also expanded Canada's markets within the British Empire and laid the foundation for both the St. Lawrence Seaway and the Reciprocity Treaty with the U.S.

Perhaps no prime minister could have done much to cure the Depression. Many historians feel that what R.B. Bennett did was too little and too late. He poured millions of dollars into relief projects and set up labour camps for the unemployed. However, he infuriated those same unemployed by imprisoning some of their leaders who were Communists.

He had also infuriated his own Cabinet ministers by not consulting them on decisions. Several did not seek re-election or ran against the Conservatives in 1935.

R.B. Bennett left Canada in 1939 to live next door to his friend Lord Beaverbrook in England. In 1941, King George bestowed upon him the title Viscount Bennett of Mickleham, Calgary and Hopewell. He died in 1947 at age 76, but his name lives on in the name of the law firm he founded, Bennett Jones. His name has also been immortalized through a strange vehicle of the Depression period: a horse-drawn motor car with its engine removed, nicknamed the "Bennett Buggy."

Pat Burns

If any Canadian ever deserved the title of Cattle King, it was Patrick Burns. From his home south of Calgary, he built up one of the world's biggest meat-packing businesses. And it all started with two oxen.

As a young man Pat Burns was working in the woods of northern Ontario. When his employer couldn't pay the $100 in wages he had earned, Pat settled for a yoke of oxen. On the hoof, they were worth $70, but by slaughtering them and selling the meat, he made $140. That was in 1878. Fifty years later he sold his interest in P. Burns and Co. Ltd. for $15 million!

Pat Burns was born in 1856 in Oshawa, Ontario, one of 10 children of Irish immigrants (whose name had been "O'Byrne" in the old country). When he was 22, he and one of his brothers struck out for Manitoba. There he worked as a farmhand and later became a homesteader who dabbled in cattle dealing and supplying beef to railway crews as far away as the state of Maine.

He was quick to recognize the business potential of the railway. Five carloads of hogs he sent from Manitoba to Ontario comprised the first shipment of western livestock to eastern Canadian markets.

In 1890, with a growing reputation as a cattle dealer and meat supplier, Pat Burns headed west again. He settled near Calgary and began building the Burns meat-packing empire in earnest. That first year he started a small slaughterhouse in Calgary. He shipped cattle into the Crowsnest Pass area, to the Kootenays and into the British Columbia interior. The Dominion government also awarded him a contract to supply meat to the Blood reserve at Sarcee.

With his brother Dominic, he began shipping meat to the Yukon, establishing depots and retail stores along the way. Then the expansion turned eastward again. Packing plants were built in Regina, Prince Albert and Winnipeg to go along with those in Calgary, Edmonton, Vancouver and Seattle. Eventually the Burns interests expanded to Montreal and Great Britain, and there was even a Burns representative in Japan. Yet Pat Burns had never received

much schooling, and many of his
deals were made with little more
than a handshake and a few notes
scribbled on the back of an envelope.

One writer described Pat Burns as
"small, round, pink and white." Yet he
was rugged enough for the unsettled
prairie, where enormous cattle herds
ranged winter and summer over
unfenced land. The man people
called the "Cattle King of the West"
also had a big heart. Once, when he
was having the small Catholic church
at Midnapore painted, he instructed

the crew to spruce up the neighbouring Anglican church as well.
With the other members of the "Big Four" of Alberta cattle-raising,
he put up the money to launch the Calgary Stampede.

Among his legions of friends were the legendary Father Albert
Lacombe and Prime Minister R.B. Bennett. Although Burns was a
Liberal, the Conservative prime minister named him to the Senate
in 1931. Earlier he had turned down both a Senate appointment
and a knighthood to concentrate on business. The appointment he
did accept was announced on his 75th birthday. The party that day
was one of Canada's most gala functions ever. The City of Calgary
proclaimed July 6 to 11 as "Burns Week." The Calgary Stampede
hosted the party. The dignitaries included the prime minister, two
premiers, two lieutenant-governors and two railway presidents. A
"Cake for a King," which weighed 1360 kilograms, was displayed and
distributed. The city prepared an illuminated plaque that read, in
part: "Western hospitality has been defined and crystallized in your
genial personality; private benevolence has received its greatest
encouragement from your unselfish liberality." Pat Burns responded
to these tributes by donating 2000 beef roasts to needy families and
2000 meal vouchers to single unemployed men. He died in 1937.

William Irvine

Alberta politics has seldom followed the Canadian pattern. Much of the difference came from the Progressive Movement, which was a source for two existing national parties, the Social Credit Party and the New Democratic Party (which grew out of the Co-operative Commonwealth Federation).

One of the midwives at the birth of the CCF in 1932 was William Irvine, a Calgary clergyman born in 1888 in the Shetland Islands. This "political evangelist" had been lured to Canada in 1908 by the missionary father of James S. Woodsworth, another clergyman who later became leader of the CCF. Bill Irvine was a Presbyterian, but switched to the Methodist Church to get permission to marry while still a divinity student. As a student minister, he worked in the lumber camps of northern Manitoba. After ordination, his rather unorthodox views resulted in a charge of heresy. Although he was acquitted, he felt stifled by the Methodist Church. He accepted a position in Calgary as a Unitarian minister. Here he had the freedom to engage in political activity.

Irvine edited a newspaper called *The Nutcracker*. When he joined the farmers' political action group known as the Non-Partisan

League in 1917, the paper was renamed the *Alberta Non-Partisan*. Two years later, the league joined the United Farmers of Alberta, which formed the provincial government from 1921 to 1935. Eventually, Irvine's paper became the *Western Independent*.

In 1921, he was elected as a Labour member of the House of Commons representing a Calgary riding. The only other Labourite elected that year was the Rev. J.S. Woodsworth. Irvine told the Commons, "The Hon.

Member for Central Winnipeg, Mr. Woodsworth, is the leader of the labour group—and I am the group."

Irvine was defeated in 1925, but was re-elected the next year as a UFA candidate in Wetaskiwin. He became part of the "Ginger Group," an independent group of MPs within the Progressive Party.

As a parliamentarian, he was described by D. Walter Thomson in the *Edmonton Journal* in 1931: "Robust and aggressive in debate, he stands erect with his raven-haired head thrown well back and in a dry, humorous way broadcasts his wordy stones and arrows of satiric logic."

He was defeated again in 1935 and spent the next nine years on his farm in Wetaskiwin. But he was re-elected in 1945, this time as CCF member for Cariboo in British Columbia. In 1949, he retired to Wetaskiwin.

William Irvine's political views were considered by some to be as unorthodox as his religious views. In 1923, he had been instrumental in bringing Major Clifford H. Douglas to explain his Social Credit theory to the Commons banking committee. Irvine, however, could never buy the Alberta brand of Social Credit advanced by Premier William Aberhart.

Throughout his political career, Irvine also opposed what he felt was an anti-democratic tendency in the Canadian parliamentary system. He wrote several books and two plays with socialist themes. In 1956, he visited the Soviet Union, and in 1960 he travelled to China. He returned with praise for the Chinese political system.

When he died in 1962, the *Lethbridge Herald* concluded an editorial tribute with these words: "No other eulogy is needed, really, and it is probable that no other would have pleased Irvine himself so greatly: he was a member of the Ginger Group."

Elizabeth Sterling Haynes

Live theatre in Alberta owes more to Elizabeth Sterling Haynes than to any other person. In fact she has been called "the spirit mother of theatre in Alberta." For 32 years this tall, energetic actress-director coaxed theatre companies into existence and travelled the province introducing people to a new outlet for their creativity.

Born in England, Elizabeth Sterling Haynes was educated in Ontario. At the University of Toronto she made her mark as a gifted actress. In 1923, she came to Edmonton with her dentist husband. A chance encounter with a former U of T professor on an Edmonton street corner led to her first directing assignment here. It was the University of Alberta production of *Dear Brutus*.

In 1928, she helped establish the Alberta Drama League. Five years later she was appointed provincial drama director for the University of Alberta Extension Department. Kilometre after gruelling kilometre, she would travel around Alberta by train, bus and car. Some years she logged as many as 21,000 kilometres. Every place she visited, people flocked to hear her talk about stagecraft and production techniques, and to ask her advice about how to develop live theatre in their communities.

A crazy dream began to come true in 1934, when the Banff School of the Theatre opened. Only 25 students had been expected, but 200 showed up. Quite a handful for Haynes and one other instructor! That school went on to become the world-famous Banff School of Fine Arts.

In the meantime Haynes applied her talents and energy to developing theatre in Edmonton as well. She was a founder of the Edmonton Little Theatre, the Women's Theatre, the Studio Theatre and the Dominion Drama Festival. "She didn't mind killing herself, or others, for theatre," said playwright Park Gowan, a friend of Haynes.

She also chaired the drama section of Alberta's Allied Arts Council and sat on the Edmonton recreation commission. In 1945, she was elected to the Edmonton Public School Board.

Her production of *Othello* for the Studio Theatre won the Calvert Trophy at the 1953 Dominion Drama Festival. Numerous other productions she had assisted picked up various awards over the years. Her students and co-workers have made significant contributions to theatre in Alberta and elsewhere.

Elizabeth Sterling Haynes left Edmonton in 1955 and died two years later in Toronto. In a tribute years later, Dr. W.G. Hardy said, "Her influence on the artistic life of this province was pervasive and enduring." The number of theatre companies now operating in Alberta confirms that opinion.

John W. Barnett

Alberta's teachers are now part of a strong organization that bargains for their rights. That organization, the Alberta Teachers' Association, owes much of its present strength to the work of one man. John Walker Barnett championed teachers' rights in Alberta from the time he got his first teaching position in a rural schoolhouse in 1911 to his death in 1947.

Barnett was born in Grantham, Lincolnshire, England. His father was a wheelwright and a lay Methodist preacher. John went to Grantham Wesleyan School and Grantham Technical Institute. He

became an apprentice teacher, and graduated from the Westminster Teacher Training College, London, in 1902. Barnett taught in England for the next nine years and became president of a branch of the National Teachers' Union. In Canada, Barnett taught first at Lougheed, later at Alberta College and at Strathcona High School. While at Strathcona, he was supervisor of music for all Edmonton schools. In 1917, he became secretary of the Alberta Teachers' Association. In 1920, he went to work for the association fulltime.

Buoyed by his union experiences in England, John set out to build a strong teachers' organization in Alberta. He envisioned an organization that would raise teaching from the status of a trade to that of a true profession. His goal was to ensure teachers' rights to material well-being through respectable salaries, achieved through collective bargaining. He also wanted teachers to have security of tenure, right of appeal in the case of dismissal, transfer or demotion as well as freedom from exploitation and other rights. Barnett fought for these rights with trade union tactics.

His efforts on behalf of both teacher welfare and the quality of education won him the respect of many for whom he worked. In 1931, he was elected president of the Canadian Teachers' Federation. His formal recognition included an honorary Doctor of Laws degree from the University of Alberta, conferred upon him posthumously at the 1947 fall convocation.

William Aberhart

On August 23, 1935 Alberta voters made history. In record numbers, they turned out to elect the world's first government based on a strange economic theory called Social Credit. They also chose as premier a man who wasn't even a candidate in the election: William Aberhart, known by the nickname of "Bible Bill."

William Aberhart had come to Alberta from Ontario in 1910 as a schoolteacher. For 20 years after 1915 he ruled with a strict hand as principal of Calgary's Crescent Heights High School. A teacher who once worked for him described him as "...a great noise and a great light. In his presence, one felt as if one were near a magnesium flare."

There was more to William Aberhart than his teacher's profession. He was also a devout Christian of fundamentalist beliefs. As a child he had imitated evangelistic preachers by pounding pine stumps in his parents' farmyard. Between 1911 and 1925, he went from the Presbyterian Church to the Methodist, and finally to the Baptist Church. As a lay preacher at Westbourne Baptist Church in Calgary, he organized large and popular Bible classes. Later he started his own religious training school, the Prophetic Bible Institute. He also discovered the power of a new invention, radio, for putting across his message. By 1935 his weekly "Back to the Bible Hour" had a radio audience of over 350,000.

In the meantime, "Bible Bill" had discovered Social Credit, the economic theory of an English engineer named Major C.H. Douglas. Its principle was the creation of "new" money to combat the power of the minority, which controlled the world's money system. Canada was in the midst of the Great Depression, and William Aberhart saw in Social Credit a solution to widespread poverty.

Fundamentalist religion and Social Credit money theories became mixed in his broadcasts. His Bible study classes became Social Credit study groups—1600 of them across Alberta. In 1935 he handpicked Social Credit candidates for every constituency in the province. On August 23, Aberhart's candidates won in 56 of the 63 ridings.

William Aberhart was a large man, over six feet tall and weighing 260 pounds. His bald head and round glasses made him a favourite subject for political cartoonists. His own sense of humour sometimes fooled his opponents into underestimating the seriousness of his mission. The people of Alberta took him seriously and saw him as their spokesman against the "big money" interests of eastern Canada.

In turn, bankers and businessmen detested Social Credit theories. Canadian courts outlawed various pieces of Alberta legislation. The lieutenant-governor considered throwing the premier out of office after Government House was closed down. Most of the press was against him.

Still, the biggest opposition came from within the ranks of the Social Credit Cabinet, from "insurgents" who felt the premier wasn't doing enough to put Major Douglas' theories into practice.

Social Credit formed the government of Alberta until 1971, chiefly under William Aberhart's friend and former student, Ernest C. Manning. "Bible Bill," however, did not live to see the end of what he had begun. He died in Vancouver in 1943. His widow insisted he be buried there rather than in Alberta, where they had been quite unhappy for years.

Charles Sherwood Noble

The hot, dry winds of southern Alberta present farmers with a serious problem. If the land is overworked and loses its moisture, the rich topsoil simply blows away. One man, Charles Sherwood Noble, spent a lifetime developing new farming techniques and equipment to overcome that problem.

Charles Noble was born in the United States in 1873. By the time he died 84 years later, he was known as one of Canada's most outstanding agricultural conservationists. Above all, he was a farmer. In 1903, he filed for a homestead at Claresholm, opened a butcher shop and became the local dealer for Massey-Harris farm equipment. The next year he sold both shop and dealership to buy 200 hectares of land from the Hudson's Bay Company.

That was the beginning. He dreamed of creating a huge "bonanza farm" like those he had seen in the U.S. By 1916, he was operating six farms, and the next year his land holdings went up to a massive 12,141 hectares. His crops were also remarkable. In different years his yields of flax, oats and wheat set world records. By 1922, however, a series of crop failures ended with the loss of his land to the mortgage companies.

"Charlie" Noble simply started again. Eight years later he was once more considered one of Alberta's biggest and best grain growers. Still, there was the problem of those hot, dry winds. It was a problem that became acute in the Dust Bowl days of the 1930s.

That is where Charles Noble the inventor came in. He had developed the Noble Drill, a machine used for planting. He had been an early supporter of the ideas of "strip farming" and of leaving a "trash cover" of weeds and stubble to keep unplanted fields from drying out. His Noble Foundation was selling brine-treated registered seed around the world.

Then, in 1936, he developed the Noble Blade, a special plow that made him famous worldwide. It was a long blade that was pulled underground, cutting off the roots of weeds. It did not disturb the surface of the soil the way traditional plows did, and so the risk of water loss was lessened.

The Noble Blade became widely used in many countries, and was manufactured in the town of Nobleford until 1998.

Leonard Brockington

An eloquent voice that became famous around the world was the trademark of a Welsh-born Calgary lawyer named Leonard Walter Brockington. The son of a rural schoolteacher, "Brock" taught briefly before coming to Canada in 1912. He had already distinguished himself as a classics scholar at the University of Wales.

A short stint as a newspaper reporter in Edmonton earned him enough to begin studying law. In 1913, he went to work with the

Calgary firm of Lougheed and Bennett. He left after a few years because he couldn't stand the junior partner, R.B. Bennett. The feeling, apparently, was mutual. All through law school he took top honours, including the gold medal of the Alberta Law Society. Later he was named King's Counsel by both Alberta and Manitoba. In 1921, he became city solicitor for Calgary, a post he held until 1935. That year he became general counsel for the North

West Grain Dealers' Association. He rapidly developed a reputation as a brilliant lawyer and an enormously popular speaker. The Toronto *Globe and Mail* called him "a veritable encyclopedia of English poetry." His wit became legend, and Leonard Brockington stories are still being told in certain quarters.

In 1936, he was named first chairman of the Canadian Broadcasting Corporation. It was a controversial appointment, since he had no previous radio experience. One of his policies remains in effect, however: free air time for opposing views on controversial issues.

During World War II, Leonard Brockington worked as special advisor to Prime Minister King. He travelled Canada, Britain, Australia and the U.S. promoting the Commonwealth war effort, particularly the role of Canada. "Our place is not where words are spoken," he said in one speech chiding the Americans for not joining the war. "Our place is where things are done."

In 1942, he was appointed advisor on Commonwealth affairs to Britain's Ministry of Information. His voice became one of the best known on radio throughout the English-speaking world. He was often on the battlefronts of Europe, despite the crippling arthritis that had afflicted him since his days as a young lawyer.

After the war he specialized in arbitrating labour disputes, including one between the U.S. government and its employees at the United Nations. He was also Rector of Queen's University from 1947 until his death in 1966.

Leonard Brockington earned scores of tributes during his lifetime. The one he cherished most was an honorary degree from the University of Wales. It was presented in 1953, the same day the new Queen Elizabeth received a similar honour.

When he accepted a Canada Council Medal in 1963, the citation called him "the greatest Canadian exponent of the art of rhetoric in our time." He had also been called "the best after-dinner speaker in Canada." In addition, he was known as an adjudicator of music and drama festivals, an accomplished amateur actor and even an occasional symphony conductor!

To his vast audiences in wartime he was the "Evangelist of Empire." To the Sarcee Indians he was "Chief Yellow Head Coming-Over-The-Hill" for his shaggy mane of blond hair. To one Calgary client he was "the man who looks like Highland cattle." Bent over from arthritis, puffing expensive cigar smoke like his good friend Winston Churchill, "Brock" would have laughed at the comparison. The advice he often gave others was, "Never neglect the merry heart."

Georges Bugnet

The word "culture" can be used in many different senses. In the case of Georges Bugnet, it sums up a life dedicated to literature, public service and the development of new plant varieties.

Georges-Charles-Jules Bugnet was born in Chalons-sur-Saone, in 1879, in the French province of Burgundy. He received a classical education at the Sorbonne and the University of Dijon. He worked as a newspaper editor in France before coming to Canada in 1904 with his young wife, Julia. He had been lured here by the prospect of making $25,000 in a few years and returning to France a wealthy man. In 1979, at the age of 100, he smiled and said, "I'm still waiting to make that $25,000."

He may not have made much money, but the cultural value of his contributions is beyond measure. His novels are considered among the greatest ever produced by a western Canadian francophone. They include *Nipsya*, about a young Cree girl and the conflicts faced by First Nations people and Métis during the Riel Rebellion, and *La Forêt*, about the hardships of life in the Canadian wilderness. A book of verse, *Voix de la Solitude*, was reissued after 40 years in 1978 to coincide with Bugnet's 99th birthday.

A school trustee for 47 years, his dedication to education was legendary. He once walked 32 kilometres in mud to catch a train for Edmonton to persuade Premier Aberhart to grant more money to his school district.

Also a noted horticulturist, he developed a world-famous variety of wild rose, named the Thérèse Bugnet after a favourite sister. This development took 25 years of patient experimenting, beginning with a cross between a Siberian double wild rose and the traditional Alberta wild rose. He also introduced a hardy Russian variety of Scots pine, the Lagoda pine, into Alberta, where it has served as an excellent windrow tree.

Georges Bugnet spent most of his life on a farm in Rich Valley near Legal, northwest of Edmonton. That farm is now an Alberta Historic Site and a source of valuable Lagoda pine seeds.

The author-educator-horticulturalist was also founder and president of the Association Canadienne-Française de l'Alberta. Throughout his life his works brought him many honours. One was the title of Chevalier dans l'Ordre des Palmes Academiques, presented by the French government in 1951. In 1979, the University of Alberta conferred upon him an honorary doctorate. The special convocation, in a church in Legal, was the first the university had conducted away from its own campus.

From his wheelchair the 99-year-old man, almost blind and deaf, told the audience he had had a "magnificent" life. Then, with the serenity that comes as a full life nears its end, he compared death to a dragonfly as it sheds its casing in the sun and "emerges into a beautiful world it had not known before."

Bugnet died in 1981, at the age of 101. In the late 1990s, he was honoured (along with the Thérèse Bugnet rose) as part of a historical mural project in Legal.

1939–

1947

Abroad & Home...

The rains and the war came in 1939.

Albertans found themselves caught up in a prosperity that gave them markets abroad and a direct role in North American defence.

The Pacific Staging Route brought American troops and planes through Alberta and the momentum of those years continued with the first big strike in oil.

Alberta was underway.

George R. Pearkes

Berkhamsted Farm, near Red Deer, was set up by an English headmaster to train British lads for prairie farming. One of its "graduates" later became an outstanding military leader, a federal Cabinet minister and lieutenant-governor of British Columbia. George Randolph Pearkes was 18 when he arrived in 1906. He was athletic and loved the outdoors. After two years at what local residents called the "Baby Farm," he began to work for various farmers in the area. One of them introduced him to Conservative politics, which played a major role in his later life.

George and his brother Edward decided to try their luck at homesteading near Rocky Mountain House. They worked hard and George took freight-hauling jobs to make ends meet. He also worked briefly with a Dominion Land Survey crew north of Fort McMurray. Here he developed an admiration for the Royal North-West Mounted Police.

The two brothers, along with their mother and sister, decided in 1912 that they couldn't make a go of it on the farm. George enlisted in the Mounties and was posted to the Yukon. Then, in 1914, when war broke out in Europe, George immediately enlisted in the 2nd Canadian Mounted Rifles. Within four years he was Lt. Col. George R. Pearkes. He had been wounded in battle five times. One bomb had injured him in eight separate places. Also, he had earned the highest military honours in the Empire—the Victoria Cross (VC), Distinguished Service Order (DSO) and the Military Cross (MC)—as well as the Croix de Guerr, awarded by the government of France.

George Pearkes remained in the army and achieved the rank of major general. In World War II he commanded the 1st Canadian Division overseas from 1940 to 1942. Then he was put in charge of Canada's Pacific Command. Soon after being relieved of that post in 1945 he was elected to the House of Commons as a Conservative. He was re-elected in the elections of 1949, 1953, 1957 and 1958. George Pearkes seemed the natural choice for Minister of National Defence in the Diefenbaker government. He held the post from 1957 to 1960.

Some critics felt he was too influenced by senior military personnel, and was a weak salesman for Canadian military equipment. To other observers he stood out as an unconventional defence minister who wanted to eliminate inefficiency in the armed forces and who advocated Canadian recognition of the People's Republic of China.

In 1960, he was appointed lieutenant-governor of British Columbia, a post he held until 1968. Many consider him the most popular person ever to hold that office. He retired in Victoria and died there in 1984, at the age of 96.

George Pearkes' attitude to public service was probably best expressed when he received the Pacific Command appointment in 1942. "I am not exactly accustomed to making pretty speeches," he told reporters. "But this you can say: I am supremely proud of the great honour that has been conferred upon me, and I pray God that I shall have the courage and good judgement to be worthy of that trust."

Wilf Carter

Long before Shania Twain, Tim McGraw or Travis Tritt, there was a man called Wilf Carter. He didn't sing country and western. He sang "cowboy music."

Wilf Carter was a cowboy, although he was born in Nova Scotia, one of nine children of a poor Baptist minister. When he was 12, Wilf came to Alberta as a field hand and his life as a singing cowboy began. For a time he lived in a deserted shack near Carbon, with a mongrel dog for company. He skinned coyotes for his "living money" and spent the rest of his time composing songs and practising the cowboy yodel that became his trademark. That yodel had been part of him from the age of 10 when he had paid a day's wages, 25 cents, to hear a singer called "The Yodelling Fool."

As a cowboy he worked at the Calgary Stampede. One of his jobs was "eardowning," or biting the ears of wild horses to calm them for saddling. While competing in the 1931 Stampede, Wilf began singing on a Calgary radio station for $5 a show. Soon afterward the CPR hired him to sing on trail rides and later on one of its cruise ships. His show business career had started.

One thing led to another. A demo record he made in Montreal was released and gained some popularity. On one side was "The Capture of Albert Johnson" and on the other was "My Swiss Moonlight Lullaby." Both songs had been written in Alberta. By 1934 he was a star on CBS Radio, with his own daily show carried over 250 stations. He received 10,000 fan letters a week. While he was in New York with that show, he met and married a nurse named Bobbie Bryan. They bought a 320-acre cattle ranch near Calgary.

A car accident in Montana in 1940 took Wilf Carter out of the singing business for nine years. He had made so many records before that, however, that the record company just kept releasing new ones as if he were still active. Wilf Carter's singing style attracted many imitators. In the United States, where he was known as Montana Slim, some singers even used his name.

In 1949, the real Wilf Carter took the stage once again. For the next four decades he was among Canada's most beloved touring acts. At his peak, he attracted 70,000 fans during a one-week run in Toronto. His recording catalogue grew to more than 40 titles. In 1991, at age 86, he completed his final tour, "The Last Roundup." A documentary featuring Wilf Carter and this tour was released in 2000.

Wilf never learned to read music, but he composed hundreds of his own songs. He was elected to the Nashville Country Music Hall of Fame, the National Cowboy Hall of Fame in Oklahoma City, the Canadian Country Music Association Hall of Fame and the Juno Awards Hall of Fame.

Wilf Carter passed away in 1996, but the songs of this tall, smiling Nova Scotia cowboy are still popular around the world, especially in England, France and Australia.

Grant McConachie

In the early days of aviation, the canvas-covered biplanes had to be wiped down after every flight. Around Edmonton, the job often went to "that freckle-faced kid who used to hang around the airport."

George William Grant McConachie didn't just hang around the airport. He lived next door. And his love of planes carried him to the top of one of the world's major airlines. Born in 1909 in Ontario, Grant came to Edmonton as a baby. In 1930, the 21-year-old pilot was headed for China to fly for a small airline. An uncle talked him out of the idea by buying him a Fokker aircraft for $2500. Independent Airways, Ltd. had begun. Chief pilot: Grant McConachie. His first cargo consisted of 800 crows, their tails painted yellow for migration experiments. Bad weather forced the plane down, and curious farmers shot the crows. Independent Airways was not off to a flying start.

In 1932, Grant McConachie broke his ankles, kneecaps, ribs and wrists in a crash near Edmonton. He later married the nurse who looked after him, Margaret MacLean. In the tough tradition of bush pilots, he went back to work long before the doctors said he should, using a long-handled axe as a crutch on treacherous northern ice. Later, with a Russian prince and princess as financial backers, he became the "Flying Fish-Packer." In 160 days, he flew over a million pounds of fresh Alberta whitefish from northern lakes to the nearest rail line. From there they were sped to hungry American markets.

All through the Depression years, Grant McConachie went on borrowing money, investing his profits in new planes, hiring more pilots. He picked up mail contracts from the federal government; he flew over 200 "mercy" flights; he carried every kind of cargo imaginable, from sled dogs to fresh vegetables. A network of tiny airstrips throughout Alberta, British Columbia, the Yukon and Northwest Territories was built for Grant McConachie. His name became known in every hamlet in the North.

During World War II he managed the observer school at Portage La Prairie, Manitoba. He also supervised the opening of a vital northwest air route used to supply planes from the U.S. across Siberia to the Russian allies.

In 1942, his career took a completely different course. He helped bring together several small bush air companies, including his own Yukon Southern Air Transport, into one large organization. It was bought by Canadian Pacific Railways and became CP Air. Grant McConachie became its western general manager and in 1947 was named president of the company.

Under his leadership, CP Air became the seventh-largest airline in the world, sending its planes into Europe, the Orient and South America.

Until his death in 1965 Grant McConachie was known as a first-class airline administrator, at home anywhere in the world. But at heart he always remained the daring bush pilot his friends had once called "the human airplane."

Hedwig Bartling

Canadians of Japanese ancestry had a tough time during World War II. Many other Canadians viewed them with suspicion and contempt because Canada was at war with Japan. The federal government uprooted Japanese-Canadians living in British Columbia and moved them inland. Businesses were destroyed—even those belonging to second- and third-generation Canadian families. Many of the West Coast evacuees were relocated to the countryside of southern Alberta, in the Lethbridge and Taber area. There they were fortunate to meet a United Church missionary who treated them with dignity and compassion.

Hedwig Dorothea Henriette Bartling understood discrimination. She had felt its sting in Saskatoon as a young girl who had recently arrived from Germany. She grew up determined to do something about it. After teacher training in Saskatchewan, she taught in that province for five years. However, she felt some training in social work would permit her to better serve the community. Although she had been brought up as a Lutheran, she enrolled in the United Church Training School in Toronto.

She went on to take a diploma in social work at the University of Toronto. In her spare time she taught English to Hungarian immigrants. In 1933, she was engaged by the Women's Missionary Society of her adopted church to work among the Ukrainian people of northeastern Alberta. After seven years of preaching and teaching and practical nursing, she entered the University of British Columbia where she received a B.A. in history in 1942.

That was the year the Japanese-Canadians were evacuated. Hedwig Bartling went to Lethbridge under the auspices of the Southern Alberta Presbytery to work among these dislocated "Nisei" people. She quickly gained their confidence and respect. For the rest of the war she helped them adjust to their new life as dryland farmers, forbidden to live in the city. She organized camps, sporting events, dances and public speaking competitions. Her aim was to help the young people, especially, develop confidence and skills in community leadership.

These efforts frequently brought her into conflict with the authorities. RCMP security personnel grilled her about what she was teaching the "XBCs" (ex-British Columbians). But Hedwig Bartling was no respecter of arbitrary power. She encouraged young Nisei girls to work in the city as maids, in defiance of the regulations. Discrimination ran high against the evacuees and against the friend they called "Barty." For some time, the only accommodation she could get was a small basement suite.

After the war, Hedwig Bartling quietly returned to BC. She worked with a Chinese mission in Victoria and later with the returning Japanese evacuees. She was ordained in 1963 and worked as a minister until 1970. Even after her retirement to Vancouver, she kept busy with hospital visiting and other church work.

When the University of Lethbridge granted her an honorary doctorate in 1980, the Japanese-Canadian community there remembered her affectionately. Wrote one member: "...the quality of civic responsibility exercised by the Japanese-Canadians today is due largely to the kind of treatment they received from a small minority of understanding people...I count the Rev. H.D. Bartling as foremost and most outstanding among all these."

Donald Cameron

The weed problems of central Alberta farmers led to the development of the Banff School of Fine Arts. The catalyst was Donald Cameron.

As a young agriculture student at the University of Alberta, Don Cameron spent his summers as a field supervisor for the provincial Department of Agriculture. In the summer evenings he heard farm families talk about their need for cultural activities, and the seed of a dream was sown.

Donald Cameron was born in England in 1903, the son of a British Admiralty engineer. The family moved to Hong Kong, where Donald learned to speak Chinese by the time he was three. The promise of land and instant wealth lured the family to western Canada in 1906. Donald's father quickly became immersed in Alberta politics. He helped found the Non-Partisan League and later sat in the Alberta legislature as the United Farmers member from Innisfail from 1921to 1935.

Donald shared his father's interests, serving as the UFA's junior president from 1921 until he went off to college in 1926. The day he graduated, the University of Alberta Extension Department hired him as lecturer and agricultural secretary. In 1932, he won a Carnegie travel scholarship to Scandinavia. The folk schools of Denmark particularly impressed him.

In 1936, Donald Cameron succeeded Dr. E.A. Corbett as director of extension and director of what had become the Banff School of Fine Arts. From then until his retirement in 1969, he spared no efforts to enrich his "Campus in the Clouds." He involved himself in every aspect of the school's growth, even to the point of designing its floor plans. With Eric Harvie he scouted out the ideal site, then coaxed the National Parks Board to let him have it. He launched exhaustive fund-raising drives, "rattling my tin cup over the highways and byways of Canada."

The school, of course, grew into one of the world's major cultural centres. In 1952, Donald Cameron also founded the Banff School of Advanced Management, which has since developed an international stature of its own.

Donald Cameron earned his spurs as a superb administrator. In 1955, he was named to the Senate of Canada, but accepted that honour only after being assured he could continue his work at Banff.

In the Senate, too, Donald Cameron earned an impressive reputation, particularly as vice-chairman of the Senate Committee on Science Policy. He was active in numerous organizations, including the Commonwealth Parliamentary Association. In 1958, he was asked to chair a provincial Royal Commission on Education. His most memorable accomplishment, however, was the flowering of a dream in the mind of a young field supervisor years ago.

Donald Cameron died in 1989. In his honour, the main administration building at the Banff Centre was renamed Donald Cameron Hall.

Matthew Halton

August 27, 1944.

"This is Matthew Halton of the CBC speaking from Paris... I am telling you about the liberation of Paris, about our entry into Paris yesterday, and I don't know how to do it...Yesterday was the most glorious and splendid day I've ever seen."

That broadcast from the Scribe Hotel in Paris was relayed through Britain and heard across Canada. It told of the end of Nazi rule in France. And it was the finest moment in the career of Canada's finest war correspondent.

Matthew Henry Halton was born in Pincher Creek in 1904. He taught school near Claresholm for a brief period before earning a scholarship to the London School of Economics. After studying there and at King's College, he returned to Canada in 1931 and joined the *Toronto Star*. The next year his paper sent him back to London to cover English and European politics. For eight years, as storm clouds grew over Germany, he reported the political weather of Europe.

As early as 1934, he warned that Germany was heading toward war. The year before he had been scared out of Germany by threats resulting from his outspoken reports. In 1940, the *Star* brought him back to North America as its Washington correspondent. He dined on sausage and eggs with President Franklin Delano Roosevelt the night he defeated Wendell Wilkie.

The war Halton had predicted was now underway. He was sent to cover the African campaign of Field Marshal Montgomery. From that experience came Halton's book, *Ten Years to Alamein*, considered among the best books to come out of World War II. Before it was published, the CBC hired Halton as a war correspondent.

Halton's reports were those of an eyewitness—clear, often emotional, but always honest. He covered the campaign in Sicily and the D-Day landing on the beaches of Normandy that led to the liberation of Paris and the eventual end of Hitler's Nazis.

After the war Matthew Halton became the CBC's chief European correspondent. He was as comfortable interviewing world leaders as he had been speaking with foot-soldiers during the war. His conversations read like a history of 20th-century public affairs—Winston Churchill, Albert Einstein, Charles de Gaulle, George Bernard Shaw, Dwight Eisenhower, Marshal Tito, Mahatma Gandhi, Haille Selassie, Pandit Nehru and so on.

He had also once argued with Adolph Hitler's lieutenant, Hermann Goering, "until we were both blue in the face." That was in 1938, the year he made the first live radio report from Munich to North America. Matthew Halton was a war correspondent who hated the horrors of war. His philosophy was expressed succinctly near the end of his book on the African campaign: "Idealism is the only realism."

When Matthew Halton died in 1956, the *Lethbridge Herald*, the first paper for which he had written remembered him: "He was a realist, and interpreted the European scene as he saw it and felt it."

His journalistic legacy continued in the form of his son, David Halton, who worked for the CBC for 40 years, much of that time as a foreign correspondent.

Chester Ronning

For many Albertans, English is a second language. For Chester Ronning, it was the third. The distinguished diplomat, author and politician was born in Fancheng, Hupeh Province, China in 1894. Hence his first language. "I spoke only Chinese at age six," he says.

His parents were Lutheran missionaries and his mother, from Norway, taught him his second language, Norwegian.

The family was forced out of China by the Boxer Rebellion of 1900 and fled to Iowa. Only then did Chester Ronning begin to speak English, and somewhat reluctantly: "I didn't like to learn a third language just to play with the other kids."

The family soon returned to China, but Chester and his brother, Nelius, immigrated to Alberta in 1907 after their mother died. They homesteaded near Camrose until 1921, when Chester and his brothers moved to the Peace River country to taste the cowboy life. The next year the call of China proved too strong for Chester, and he went off to study in Peking. His love affair with China and its people never ended. Although not a communist, he admired the social experiment being conducted by Chairman Mao Tse-tung. Chester Ronning's voice was one of the first raised to urge Canada and other western nations to recognize "Red China."

In 1932, back in Canada, he was elected to the Alberta legislature for the United Farmers of Alberta party. Three years later he attempted to become the first elected member of the CCF (which later became the New Democratic Party). He lost in the big sweep by William Aberhart's Social Credit. Chester Ronning went on to become leader of the Alberta CCF, but it was as a diplomat rather than as a politician that he made his biggest mark.

He had fought in the First World War. In World War II he became a Squadron Leader with the RCAF intelligence service. At war's end he was posted to China by the Department of External Affairs, "without any training as a civil servant, or as a diplomat, and I haven't had any training since."

In 1951, he was recalled from China, and three years later was appointed Canada's Ambassador to Norway and Iceland. He represented Canada at the Geneva conferences on Korea and Vietnam in 1954 and on Laos in 1961. He was also Canada's High Commissioner to India from 1957 to 1964.

Canada tried to negotiate a settlement of the Vietnam War in 1966. The country's hopes were tied up in one man: Chester Ronning, special envoy to Saigon and Hanoi. But he was unable to bring about peace between the United States and North Vietnam.

From the exciting life of international diplomacy Chester Ronning retired to the quiet country life of Camrose, where he died in 1984. In 1980, the National Film Board of Canada released a film about Chester Ronning, entitled "China Mission." Its director, Tom Radford, summed up his subject with these words: "This is a man whose dreams were decimated time after time. Yet each time he came back and persevered—because he never had any illusions of his own importance."

Alexander Calhoun

In 1913, the British poet Rupert Brooke made a tour of Canada. Among the things he wrote about was this country's system of public libraries. He felt they got better as one progressed westward, and the brand-new Calgary Public Library appealed to him most. "Few large English towns could show anything as good," he wrote. The credit belonged to Alexander Calhoun.

Calhoun had come to Calgary as chief librarian two years earlier, stepping off the train one February day. "I had come to organize a library," he wrote. "The balmy chinook was abroad in the land and the air was like wine." He was 31. When he died in 1979, just months short of his 100th birthday, he left behind a remarkable record of community service.

He was born in the Ontario sawmill village of Fenelon Falls. Studies in Kingston, Chicago and Winnipeg gave him solid academic credentials in Greek, English literature, political science, German and French. It was while he was teaching high school in Fort William that he helped establish a public library board.

When the members of Calgary's library board hired him for $1800 a year, they didn't know what a bargain they were getting. Calhoun quickly plunged into community activities. During the First World War, he persuaded the city to set aside vacant lots for gardens, for a rental fee of $1. Immediately over 1500 gardens sprang up. Calhoun's respect for the "common man" included the "common woman" as well. In 1916, he joined the fight to win Alberta women the right to vote. "All my life," he said much later, "I have fought for the underdog."

Calhoun took a brief leave of absence from the library during 1918. He went to Vladivostock, Russia with the Canadian Expeditionary Force. "There we sat on our fannies, along with other allied forces," he said. "It was all a complete farce."

Alexander Calhoun was not one to sit on his fanny for long. He was a member of Calgary's first planning commission. He was a

charter member of the Calgary branch of the Knights of the Round Table, one of the original directors of the Canadian Library Council and first president of the Alberta Library Association.

As Calgary's Chief Librarian for 34 years, he created an impressive library system that emphasized selection and training of staff. He also believed in getting books into circulation, not stored away in "rare book" rooms.

His interests were always varied. He belonged to the Canadian Institute of International Affairs, the Canada Foundation and the Alpine Club. He was also president of the Alberta Society of Artists and first president of the Allied Arts Council in Calgary. "I have no creative gifts," he said in 1969, "only an interest in the arts because they have an important role to play in any community." As a hiker, camper and mountain climber, Calhoun remained physically active for years. The day before he turned 85 he climbed Sulphur Mountain, near Banff.

In 1987, six years after Calhoun's death, the Calgary Public Library opened the new Alexander Calhoun branch in the city's southwest.

Illingworth Kerr

Illingworth Kerr was one of Canada's foremost painters of animals and landscapes. As a teacher and painter, he also had a great deal of influence on many artists of Alberta.

Born in 1905 in Lumsden, Saskatchewan, he began drawing animals as a very young boy, encouraged by his mother, an amateur water colourist. Immediately after high school in 1924 he spent a summer as a dump wagon driver. This job gave him both the nickname "Buck" and the $100 that took him to Toronto, where he took an art course at the Central Technical School.

Financed by a generous uncle, Kerr went on to four years' study at the Ontario College of Art (1924–27). Arthur Lismer, J.E.H. MacDonald, F.H. Varley and J.W. Beatty all taught Illingworth, although none of them specifically taught the Group of Seven's approach to rendering landscapes. He also visited the studios of Lawren Harris and A.Y. Jackson. But despite his four years of art college, Kerr considered himself basically self-taught.

He returned to Lumsden in 1927 where he painted and earned a living as a farm hand, sign writer, hunter and trapper. He also

proved a talented writer, and published his works with his own illustrations.

In 1936, he went to England, where he worked on documentary films and studied at the Westminster School of Art in London. In Scotland over the next few years Kerr created his four dioramas for the Canadian government display in the Empire Exhibition at Glasgow. He and his wife travelled Europe and returned to Canada in 1939.

Kerr's early work seems representational. But after 1955, and a summer school at Hans Hoffmann School of Fine Art in Princetown, Massachusetts, his work took a turn toward the abstract. He became interested in the works of Chagall, Picasso, Braque and in totem art. But he was still grappling with the particular problems of painting prairie landscapes.

Kerr taught for several years, and headed the Alberta College of Art from 1947 to 1967. His influence created one of the most respected art schools in Canada. Kerr's accolades include an honorary PhD from the University of Calgary, and his paintings can be found in many of the major art museums and galleries across Canada.

Kerr continued as an active painter almost up until his death in 1989, at the age of 82. Even as an octogenarian, he was still known to paint landscapes, standing up for six hours or more at a time. At the time of Kerr's death, Stan Perrott, who succeeded Kerr as head of the Alberta College of Art, called him "The Mount Everest of art in Alberta."

1948-

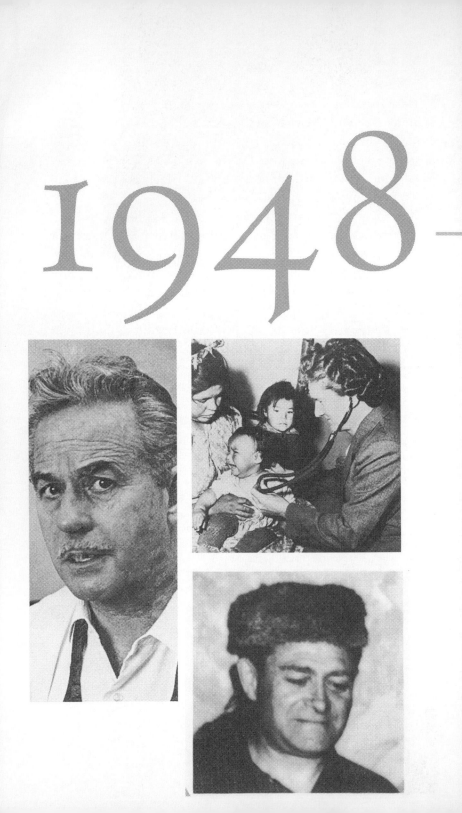

1960

The Bumper Crop...

*The farm base that had sustained
Albertans through prosperity and Depression
was now only one option among many.*

*A reverse migration into the cities
changed the rural character of Alberta
within a decade
and signalled new economic patterns.*

*The migration was also to stretch
the social fabric of a province.*

W.G. Hardy

Alberta's universities have been home to many remarkable personalities. Among the most prominent was William George Hardy, classics scholar, historian, author and hockey executive.

An Ontario farm hardly seems the ideal breeding ground for a Greek and Latin scholar. But it was while ploughing his father's fields that W.G. Hardy taught himself the Greek language. "You just buy the books," he said. He had already learned Latin, had finished public school by the age of 10 and "...used to write long, epic poems when I was 12."

Throughout his 84-year life Hardy remained an ardent scholar. His normal reading speed was 300 pages an hour, with full comprehension. As a writer he was equally fast. A short story he wrote in 1945 took him 25 minutes and earned $200. He graduated from the University of Toronto in 1917, capturing medals in classics and english as well as the Governor General's gold medal as the university's top student.

Sports were always important to George Hardy. Later in life he was president of both the Canadian Amateur Hockey Association and the International Hockey Association. He was also inducted into the Edmonton Sports Hall of Fame. Why combine sports with scholarship? "That was the Greek way of doing things," he explained. "I didn't want to become a straight academic. I was too interested in people."

While lecturing in classics at the University of Toronto he polished off a Master's degree in 1919. Three years later he received a doctorate in Greek and Roman literature from the University of Chicago. That year he became an assistant professor at the U of A, where he headed the Classics Department from 1938 to 1964.

Despite the demands of scholarship, W.G. Hardy was a prolific writer. His first novel, *Son of Eli*, was serialized in *Maclean's* magazine in 1928. It was followed by over 200 short stories and half a dozen novels, many based on Greek and Roman historical topics. One of his best novels was *The City of Libertines* (1958). Hardy also wrote a major Canadian history book, *From Sea Unto Sea* (1960), and was editor-in-chief for both the *Alberta Golden Jubilee Anthology* in 1955 and *Alberta: A Natural History* in 1967. He served three terms as president of the Canadian Authors Association.

This output was possible because of Hardy's high energy and the discipline to meet a set quota of words every day. "I write very fast," he said. "I never pretended to be a genius, but I have a talent for writing. I know my stuff." That statement was made in 1979, just months before Hardy's death at the age of 84. He had just finished the manuscript of a new historical novel, *The Bloodied Toga*, the second part of a fictional version of Julius Caesar's life.

Dr. Hardy earned many awards during his lifetime. Probably because—as he said of his brief public school career—"they just let me go at my own speed."

Clifford E. Lee

To some people a millionaire socialist might seem out of place in Alberta. Yet Clifford E. Lee was thoroughly Albertan. A month after the province came into being he was born on a farm that is now part of Edmonton's Hardisty district. He was first a teacher and later a pharmacist, but it was the house-building industry that made him a wealthy man.

Clifford Lee graduated from the Camrose Normal School in 1924. For ten years he taught in country schools. He also apprenticed with a pharmacist in Ryley for two years and decided to seek a degree in pharmacy from the University of Alberta.

Early in life, Clifford Lee had developed a keen interest in politics. He had been a member of the Tuxis Boys' Parliament. But the U of A in the early 1930s didn't allow political activity on campus, and Lee soon became part of an off-campus group of the new CCF, the left-wing party that designed the Regina Manifesto of 1933, and which later became the New Democratic Party. When the CCF newspaper *People's Weekly* began, Clifford Lee was one of its regular columnists. Later he served several terms as Alberta president of the CCF and ran unsuccessfully for the party both federally and provincially.

In the meantime, his pharmacy business in downtown Edmonton was flourishing. But Clifford Lee wasn't a typical free-enterprise pharmacist. He encouraged the people who worked for him to buy shares and become partners in his business. He also started Edmonton's first grocery co-operative, although it failed to take root.

The turning point for Clifford Lee came in 1945, when servicemen began returning to Alberta after the Second World War. The resulting housing shortage encouraged Lee to become interested in finding a way to provide housing at a reasonable price for those who needed it. Although he had no experience in house-building, he was a skilled

businessman. Using the same principle of partner-managers, he attracted other talented persons to work with him.

One such person was Ralph Scurfield. Lee took him on to manage a housing project in Thompson, Manitoba. Scurfield went on to head Nu West Homes, a small company Lee started in Calgary. Nu West prospered in the booming prairie city. It became one of the biggest housing development companies in North America. When it became a public corporation in the late 1960s, Clifford E. Lee was suddenly wealthy.

It had never been Lee's purpose to make big money from housing. Accordingly, the bulk of his profits was turned into a charitable foundation, the Clifford E. Lee Foundation. Over the years it has made substantial contributions to projects in the performing arts, social services, wildlife conservation, native concerns and international relief.

The man whose business acumen and humanitarian principles spawned this charity did not live to see his generosity bear its full fruit. Clifford E. Lee died in 1972, just three years after the foundation was established.

Laura Attrux

When Laura Attrux received an honorary doctorate from the University of Alberta in 1970, she gave some advice to the nursing graduates of that year. "Above all, become involved with people— make friends, they are your most treasured asset."

Hundreds of letters from people in northern Alberta had flooded the university in support of her nomination for the degree. All were from friends she had found in her 35 years of outpost medical service.

Laura Attrux felt as if she didn't have a friend in the world when she arrived at her first government posting in Valleyview in 1939. After living in cities such as Toronto and Calgary for 12 years, the young nurse was stricken with doubt when she surveyed that isolated Alberta community.

The landscape was a sea of mud surrounding a pitiful huddle of shacks—a small store and post office, a small cafe and a gas station. One of the community's three farm trucks grunted through the mud track that masqueraded as main street. A group of children, looking like tattered scarecrows in cast-off clothes, surrounded her in grimy-faced curiosity.

But Laura squared her shoulders, told herself "you're not a quitter," and marched through the door of the tiny cottage provided for her by the townspeople.

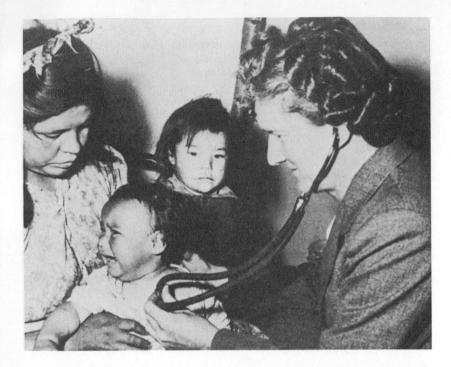

As an outpost nurse, Laura was expected to treat diseases, attend to accident injuries, provide maternity care and carry out public health work such as health education, clinics and immunization. "But we did more than that," she says. "We had to. There were no veterinarians, so we assumed that role as well, treating everything from canaries to Clydesdale horses." She was also a dentist, counsellor, social worker and community leader.

Transportation, or the lack of it, proved to be the biggest obstacle to the performance of her duties. Being resourceful, she concocted several ingenious methods of reaching her outpatients or moving the patients to a doctor or hospital. Dog teams, horses, snowshoes, skis, even a team of oxen were used in emergencies. Usually a sturdy pair of feet took her the usual two or three miles between house calls.

Laura Attrux spent two years in Valleyview, taking her services to the district homesteaders, most of them farmers who had fled Saskatchewan's dust bowl. She learned to love the country, the people, the satisfaction of her work, the sunny summers and the winter snow (but never the mud) before she moved on to a new posting at Whitecourt.

She didn't stop there either. Before Laura Attrux retired in 1974, she served the communities of Smith, Slave Lake, Wabasca, Swan Hills, Paddle Prairie, High Level and the vast regions surrounding these centres. She was one of hundreds of nurses who have worked in Alberta's isolated communities since the beginning of the Department of Public Health's district nursing division in 1919.

But unlike many others, Attrux devoted most of her life to her outpost career. Beginning it at a time when snowshoes were a major means of transportation in the wilderness and ending it at the controls of her own Cessna 150 bush plane, she managed to bridge the gap between yesterday and today.

After retiring to Edmonton, Attrux joined an informal group of retired nurses who visited the elderly, offering support and advice. In an interview in July 1987, two months before her death, she said, "For your own happiness you want to be involved with people and help in the education of people."

To the end, she gained her greatest pleasure from serving others.

Mary Percy Jackson

"The ability to ride a horse would be an advantage" was the line that caught and held Dr. Mary Percy's attention. It was part of an ad run in 1929 seeking British doctors to work in northern Alberta, and it stirred her imagination because she loved horses but rarely had the time to ride them. Understandably so. By the time she was 24, Mary Percy had graduated from the University of Birmingham with four medical degrees and a Queen's scholarship, and had worked as a house physician and house surgeon in Birmingham General Hospital.

Snared by the horses and the promise of a romantic adventure in Canada's "wild west," the prim and proper young doctor set sail for Canada in June 1929. A month later she travelled 160 kilometres north of Peace River on a river barge. When the barge landed, Mary disembarked with her 29 pieces of luggage, only to set out once more, this time on a bone-shaking 11-hour wagon ride. The temperature was 35 degrees C, and the air was thick with mosquitoes.

If any romantic notions survived her journey, they died as soon as she saw the small shack that was to be her hospital and her home. Gone were the clean, well-equipped hospitals she was used to; gone were any traces of the comforts a civilized city offers.

Mary's employer, the Alberta government, had assigned her a territory of roughly 900 square kilometres. She was equipped with basic medical supplies but no running water or electricity. The nearest medical aid was in Peace River, 120 kilometres away by dirt road.

Her only means of transportation was a saddle horse, but she had come prepared for that—or so she thought. Her first house calls were made in proper British riding clothes: breeches, boots and a riding habit. After an average 32 kilometres a day, she couldn't pull the boots from her swollen feet. Eventually moccasins and a buckskin jacket replaced the formal attire.

She delivered hundreds of babies in one-room shacks and in smoky tents, performed operations by candlelight on kitchen tables, battled tuberculosis and rabies, pulled teeth and even treated livestock. Despite the hardships, Dr. Percy fell in love with northern Alberta and its people.

In 1930, she married Frank Jackson, a farmer and rancher who shared her enthusiasm for the land. They moved farther north to Keg River. Here, though no longer under contract with the government, she continued practising medicine because "when people were ill, I couldn't refuse them." She was paid for her services in blueberries, moccasins or moose meat as none of her patients could pay cash. In fact, she received no regular pay for her work until the introduction of medicare in the 1960s.

Mary's practice in the Keg River area continued until her retirement in 1974. Somewhere in those hectic years she also managed to become an author, raise five children and take an active part in improving the standard of education in her community.

Over the years, Dr. Jackson received many awards, including the Centennial Medal of Canada, the Order of Canada and the Alberta Order of Excellence. The school near Keg River was named in her honour. In 1988, she published a memoir, *The Homemade Brass Plate*.

Jackson lived in Keg River until the mid-1990s, when she moved to Manning. She died in 2000, aged 95. In 2005, Jackson was the very first person named as one of the "100 Physicians of the Century" by the Alberta Medical Association and the College of Physicians and Surgeons of Alberta.

Earle Parkhill Scarlett

Dr. Earle Parkhill Scarlett once said, "Experience has taught us that it is the uncommon people—those with more character, more thought, more imagination and more understanding—that really guide the world."

He knew what he was talking about. In all the things he did in his life—messenger boy, store clerk, sleeping car conductor, soldier, teacher, doctor, author, scholar, university chancellor—he remained an uncommon man.

Earle Scarlett was born in 1896 in the hamlet of High Bluff, Manitoba, the son of a nomadic Methodist minister. When he turned 15, his father told him that his income, education and future were all up to him from that day onward. Deciding on an arts degree from the University of Manitoba, he supported himself with odd jobs until his graduation in 1916. He spent the next two years fighting overseas. Severely wounded in 1918, he was hospitalized for seven months before his release.

When Earle returned home, he began to consider medicine as a career. In a quiet survey of his father's friends, he found that the only men who were content with their lives were the doctors. His decision felt right and he entered the University of Toronto's Faculty of Medicine. While there he became founder and editor of North America's first undergraduate medical journal. In his spare time he became distracted by a pretty young arts graduate, Jean Odell, and married her after graduating in 1924.

After an internship in the United States, Dr. Scarlett moved to Calgary where he joined the Associate Clinic and made a home for his wife and three children. "Those were the days," he says, looking back to 1930, "when doctors cured typhoid by immersing the patient in a tub of water with ice floating in it—to bring the fever down."

Aware that there was no one documenting medical pioneering in Alberta, Dr. Scarlett began the *Calgary Associate Historical Bulletin*, which successfully recorded the now-obsolete practices of that era. The same year the *Bulletin* began, Dr. Scarlett began giving sex education classes at the YMCA, which in 1931 caused a furor of opposition—including complaints to the police.

In 1958, Scarlett retired from practising medicine and stepped down as chancellor of the University of Alberta—an office he had held since 1952. He enjoyed a long retirement in Calgary, passing away in 1982 just days short of his 96th birthday.

Earle Scarlett's life may have been controversial, but it was never dull. He attended the Baker Street Irregulars—a society devoted to the study of Sherlock Holmes. He also fought for survival of the arts in education through his role as chancellor. He did the things he believed in.

Raymond Urgel Lemieux

When Raymond Lemieux died in 2000, at the age of 80, the *Edmonton Journal* called him "the Maurice Richard of biochemistry, one of the greatest scientists Canada has ever produced."

A small northern Alberta community may have seemed an unpromising start for an internationally known scientist, but Raymond Urgel Lemieux's career didn't seem to suffer.

Lemieux was born in Lac La Biche in 1920. In 1943 he received a Bachelor of Science degree with honours in chemistry from the University of Alberta. A PhD in chemistry from McGill University followed in 1946. Post-graduate studies took him to Ohio State University where he was instrumental in determining the structure of the antibiotic, streptomycin.

Two years on the staff of the University of Saskatchewan followed before he went to work at the Prairie Regional Laboratory of the National Research Council in 1949. Four years after this appointment Lemieux successfully synthesized sucrose, common table sugar. The world's top scientists had spent over a century unsuccessfully trying to accomplish this feat, which earned him the lifelong nickname "Sugar Ray."

In 1954, Lemieux became Chairman of Chemistry and Dean of Pure and Applied Science at the University of Ottawa. Under his guidance, it became an outstanding research centre.

In 1961, Dr. Lemieux was appointed Professor of Organic Chemistry at the University of Alberta. Six years later he was named a Fellow of the Royal Society of London, the highest scientific distinction in the British Commonwealth. Lemieux was the first western

Canadian to receive the honour. Past members of the Royal Society of London include the most outstanding scientists in recent centuries, such as Isaac Newton, Michael Faraday, Charles Darwin and Joseph Lister. In 1968, Lemieux was made an Officer of the Order of Canada.

Lemieux was the U of A's Chairman of Organic Chemistry from 1966 to 1973. Scientific research, he felt, should solve real problems and have real payoffs. Lemieux had long advocated more Canadian-owned high-tech industries. He started Raylo Chemicals in 1967. He was also founder, president and research director of R & L Molecular Research Ltd. and president of Chembiomed Ltd. One of the main thrusts of Chembiomed's work was a new approach to typing human blood. A synthetic antigen was produced and used in the manufacture of a better blood typing serum. The substance has helped answer questions about differences in human blood types.

As Lemieux grew older, the professional accolades continued. He received dozens of medals, awards and honorary doctorates, culminating in the 1999 Wolf Prize in Chemistry, considered by many to be an honour equal to a Nobel Prize.

In 1998, two year's before Lemieux's death, the U of A endowed the R.U. Lemieux Chair in Carbohydrate Chemistry. Lemieux's work in the development and application of scientific knowledge will continue to have major spinoffs for decades to come.

Eric L. Harvie

He was born a dentist's son in Orillia, Ontario. At the peak of his career he was rumoured to be the richest man in Canada. He died as a person who—in the words of *Time* magazine—"gave everything back and then some."

Eric Latterly Harvie came to Calgary with his parents in 1911 when he was 19. He studied law at Osgoode Hall in Toronto and at the University of Alberta. In 1915, he joined the Calgary law firm of his uncle, J.D. Latterly, a former mayor of that city. Then the First

World War intervened. While fighting as an infantryman in 1916, he was seriously wounded at the Somme. He later joined the Royal Flying Corps.

Back in Canada, he married Dorothy Jean Southam, who came from a wealthy publishing family whose holdings included the *Calgary Herald*. Yet Eric Harvie didn't need his in-laws to provide him with financial security. In the 1920s and 30s, along with many other Calgarians, he began to dabble in land purchases around the oil fields of Turner Valley.

Dabbling turned serious in 1944 when he bought mineral rights to almost half a million acres of land around Leduc, just south of Edmonton. Stories of what he paid for that land ranged from $4850 to $110,000. The exact figure is not important, because on February 13, 1947 an oil well called Imperial Leduc No. 1 blew in and began the petroleum boom in Alberta.

The Leduc find was quickly followed by a major oil discovery at Redwater—also on land controlled by Eric Harvie. Within five years he had amassed a fortune reported to exceed $100 million.

Harvie wasn't content to sit back and watch his money grow. He began to collect things: paintings, First Nations rattles, treaties and other artifacts, British medals, arms and armour. He had a vision of

preserving the mixed cultural heritage of western Canada. Treasures bought around the world were stored in Calgary factory buildings.

In 1966, his vision matured when he presented his collection of over 200,000 items to the Alberta government, along with an endowment of $5 million. Ten years later the Glenbow-Alberta Institute was opened in downtown Calgary—a $12 million monument chronicling the development of the prairies and Alberta in particular. Sadly, Harvie passed away in 1975, a year before the museum opened.

The Glenbow was by no means the only tangible evidence of Eric Harvie's generosity. The Devonian Foundation he had established in 1956 financed a 10,120 square metre covered park in Calgary called the Devonian Gardens. It also gave money to numerous Alberta towns to spruce up their main streets.

The Calgary Zoo, Heritage Park, the Calgary Allied Arts Centre, the Fathers of Confederation Centre in Charlottetown, PEI, and the Banff School of Fine Arts also benefited from his gifts. The Scottish town of Bannockburn received a mounted statue of King Robert the Bruce, and Calgary was given a duplicate. His philanthropy was wide and varied, yet Eric Harvie preferred to remain in the shadows, in spite of his conspicuous charity.

His contribution to western Canada seemed understated in 1957 when he was presented with an honorary degree from the University of Alberta: "Mr. Harvie is one of those men who has been endowed with a sense of history and he has the energy and ability to do something about it."

W.O. Mitchell

Alberta's most popular writer wasn't an Alberta writer at all. He lived in Alberta, but W.O. Mitchell was born and raised in Saskatchewan. His best-loved novel was set in that province. Perhaps it is most accurate to describe W.O. Mitchell as an all-Canadian storyteller. But he was also a teacher and performer who once worked as a salesman, lifeguard, seaman, editor and high school principal.

William Ormond Mitchell was born in Weyburn, Saskatchewan, in 1914. His experiences during the Depression provided much of the material for his later writing. Because of a medical problem, young Billy Mitchell was taken to Florida by his family for part of his secondary education. Later he studied at the universities of Manitoba and Alberta.

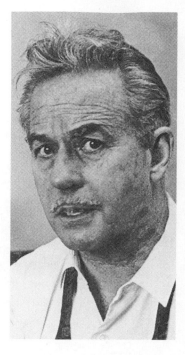

His first novel, *Who Has Seen the Wind?*, was published in 1947. It tells the story of a young boy coming to grips with the cycle of life and death. The book has been a favourite of generations of Canadian readers. It has sold over 50,000 copies a year and formed the basis of a successful motion picture.

During the 1950s, W.O. Mitchell's radio series, *Jake and the Kid*, was regular entertainment in Canadian homes from coast to coast. Several of the scripts were assembled into a book, which won the Leacock Award for humour in 1961. They also formed the basis for a successful television series in the late 1990s.

Mitchell received many tributes during his career, including the Order of Canada and honorary degrees from five Canadian universities. Another Mitchell play, *The Black Bonspiel of Wullie MacCrimmon*, was an enduring hit with theatre audiences across Canada. It tells the story of a man who makes a deal with the devil to win the country's biggest curling competition.

Mitchell described writing as "just like lying." But, he added, "when you can suspend disbelief, then it's a magic lie." W.O. Mitchell beguiled his readers into suspending their disbelief. He did it with a mixture of wry humour, accurate dialogue and distinctive twists of plot and pacing.

Mitchell worked tirelessly to inspire up-and-coming writers as well. He taught creative writing at various Canadian universities, and for years was the head of the writing program at the Banff Centre.

In the late 1980s and the early 90s, Mitchell continued to produce novels from his home in Calgary, at the rate of nearly one a year. He published his final novel, *For Art's Sake*, in 1992. He died in 1998, after a long battle with cancer.

A year earlier, in 1997, the W.O. Mitchell Literary Prize had been established to honour writers who had effectively mentored others. The announcement was made at a special tribute, with Mitchell as the honoured guest. At the ceremony in Calgary, broadcaster Peter Gzowski paid fitting tribute to Mitchell and his outstanding personal and literary legacy. "Some Canadian writers are more honoured," said Gzowski. "There are some who are richer, some who have sold more books and some who are better known around the world. But there is no writer in this country who is better loved than W.O. Mitchell."

Walter MacKenzie

Edmonton's stature as a centre for medical research is largely the result of the efforts of Dr. Walter Campbell MacKenzie. For 15 years, Dr. MacKenzie was Dean of the University of Alberta's Faculty of Medicine. His contribution to its development was such that the university's $140-million health science building bears his name.

A distinguished surgeon, Dr. MacKenzie dedicated much of his life to training other surgeons. "I'm always interested in doing anything that will improve medical service...in particular, teaching," he said. For him, research was at the core of a doctor's requirements, along with a will to work hard.

Walter Campbell MacKenzie was the son of a hotel proprietor in Glace Bay, Nova Scotia. He trained at Dalhousie, McGill and the University of Minnesota before interning in surgery for four years at the Mayo Clinic in Rochester, Minnesota. In 1938, he set up private practice in Edmonton.

The Second World War intervened and MacKenzie served six years as a surgical consultant with the Royal Canadian Navy. Then he returned to Edmonton, where he spent nine years as a professor and Chairman in the U of A Surgery Department before becoming Dean of Medicine in 1959.

His successor, Dr. D.F. Cameron, summed up Dr. MacKenzie's international reputation with the words, "From Peking to Moscow to the Arctic to the jungles of Africa, mention Edmonton and they will say. 'I have a good friend there in Walter MacKenzie.'"

Certainly MacKenzie's work brought him international recognition. He held membership in 25 medical societies and was president of half of them. He headed both the Royal College of Physicians and Surgeons of Canada and the American College of Surgeons.

Numerous honours came his way. For two years he was Honorary Surgeon to Her Majesty Queen Elizabeth. The Canadian Medical Association gave him its F.N.G. Starr Award, which is known as the "Victoria Cross of Canadian Medicine" and put him in the company of such noted Canadian doctors as Banting, Best and Penfield. Nonmedical honours included a Centennial Medal and the Order of Canada.

When he retired from the U of A in 1974, he remained active as executive director of the provincial Cancer Hospitals Board. Dr. MacKenzie was also chairman of a provincial task force on highway deaths and suicide. That group made 78 specific recommendations to reduce traffic injuries. Many were controversial, including reduced speed limits and compulsory use of seat belts. Before his death in 1978, Dr. MacKenzie became an outspoken critic of the effect of medicare on doctors' morale.

As always, at the core of this man of medicine was his devotion to research, which continued under his name in Alberta in a world-class health sciences building at the University of Alberta.

James Gladstone

Few could imagine that a young Blood First Nations boy who used beef ribs to skate on the iced-over Belly River would someday become the first aboriginal to be appointed to the Canadian Senate. Certainly not James Gladstone, known as "Many Guns" or Akay-na-muka in Blackfoot. But the courage that James showed in his early years might have indicated that great things were in store for him.

Born in Mountain Hill, in what is now Alberta, in 1887, James was sent to St. Paul's Anglican Mission School when he was seven. That first year he was tormented by a group of older boys who liked to make him the butt of their jokes. Their favourite trick was to hurl James into the graveyard when the supervisor wasn't looking. The Blood didn't bury their dead but wrapped them in blankets and placed them in the trees. At first James was terrified but, when no ghosts appeared, he got brave enough to poke through the burial bundles. Here he found two skulls that he managed to sneak into the dormitory and hang above the beds of his tormentors. The two boys fainted and several others screamed when the ghoulish relics were found.

While still a schoolboy, he helped the Royal North-West Mounted Police catch an escaped murderer. James led them to the tell-tale footprints the convict had left in the snow. At 18, perhaps in recognition of his help to them years before, the RNWMP hired him as chief scout and interpreter for their base at Fort Macleod. That same year he met and married Janie Healy, the daughter of a prominent Blood Chief.

After their marriage, James served as a mail carrier for the Blood Indian Agency. When the First World War broke out in 1914, he put large areas of the Blood Reserve into crop to help the war effort. His efforts at grain farming and cattle raising proved so successful that many Bloods followed his example and became farmers and ranchers themselves.

Janie and James had six children over the course of these uncertain years. But thanks to James' willingness to try new methods of farming, the children never went hungry. He was first on the reserve to buy a tractor. He also began using power machinery and chemical fertilizers, and was the first to have electricity in his home.

Word of Gladstone's hard work and success eventually spread throughout the province. He was voted president of the Indian Association of Alberta, a position he held for nine years. The following year James Gladstone was appointed to the Senate of Canada. He served prominently on a joint Senate-Commons committee on Indian Affairs, which led to treaty First Nations becoming eligible to vote in federal elections in 1962.

True to his name, Many Guns fought and won many battles before dying of a heart attack in 1971. Gladstone Mountain in southern Alberta is a tribute to a man who served as an example to all Canadians.

Maxwell Bates

"I am an artist, who, for forty years
Has stood at the lake edge
Throwing stones in the lake.
Sometimes, very faintly,
I hear a splash."

Maxwell Bates certainly heard a splash in 1928. The stone he had thrown into the lake was an abstract painting called *Male and Female Forms*. It was the first of its kind exhibited in Calgary. Public reaction was so hostile that Bates was expelled from the Calgary Art Club. A similar fate befell his colleague, W.L. "Roy" Stevenson. Painter and art commentator Ron Bloore called Bates and Stevenson "the most advanced painters in western Canada during this period."

Maxwell Bates was born in Calgary. He worked for his father's architectural firm in 1924 before enrolling in the Provincial Institute of Technology and Art (now the Alberta College of Art). As a painter he pioneered in the style of painting known as abstract expressionism.

In 1931, he went to England to study painting and architecture. For most of the next decade his name was associated with a school of artists known as the Twenties Group. His income from art was augmented by jobs selling water softeners and vacuum cleaners.

Max Bates enlisted in the British Army in 1939. He spent most of the Second World War as a prisoner of war working in German salt mines. In prison camp he ran art classes and got involved in camp theatre, including acting in a production of *Twelfth Night*.

He returned to Calgary in 1946 to pursue both painting and architecture. A few years later he went to New York to study at the Brooklyn Museum Art School, but came back to Calgary in 1950. His most striking creation as an architect was St. Mary's Cathedral in Calgary, which he designed with A.W. Hodges.

Bates was a master of many styles. He and another artist, John Snow, pioneered lithographic techniques in western Canada. Bates' own work in oils and watercolours often threw out normal space relationships to emphasize the psychological relationships of his subjects. Many of his paintings are considered bizarre, grotesque, gloomy or satiric, and he has been compared with a number of major artists including Picasso and Max Beckman (with whom he studied in Brooklyn). Yet the noted critic Robin Skelton called him "one of the most powerful, original and profound painters of his generation."

Maxwell Bates often turned to writing—particularly poetry—to express the currents of his thought. He advocated an openness and a naivete through which the artist could communicate the essential character of his subjects. "The naive painter," he wrote, "is a humanist making plastic comments on the residue of daily life."

A stroke in 1961 paralyzed the left side of his body, and Bates was forced to give up architecture. He retired to Victoria and continued to paint until his death in 1980.

Frank McMahon

Many fortunes have been made in Alberta through a combination of shrewd analysis, hard work and good luck. "The luck of the Irish" came through more than once for Frank McMahon.

Francis Murray Patrick McMahon was born in Moyie, British Columbia. After three years of university he worked as a diamond driller. Then he came to Turner Valley in southern Alberta. With his brothers, George and John, he started drilling for oil under the company name of West Turner Petroleums. From 1935 to 1939, the luck wasn't with them. Finally they struck it rich with a well yielding 32,000 barrels of oil a day. A holding company, Pacific Petroleums, emerged. In 1947, MacMahon bought into the huge Leduc oil field and the next year his luck really turned bad—or so it seemed.

McMahon's Atlantic No. 3 well came in with such force that it was immediately out of control. For six months it spewed oil and gas onto the countryside. The ground softened and the drilling rig collapsed, snapping electrical cables and setting off a shower of sparks. The mammoth lake of oil caught fire. For 56 hours it raged, the most spectacular well fire in Canadian history. Finally the well was plugged with a combination of coiled cable, golf balls and chicken feathers.

Enter that fabled Irish luck. The publicity brought the vast reserves of Leduc to world attention. "Pacific Pete" was flooded with offers of investment money. Frank McMahon embarked on a wildcat search for oil and gas in the Peace River area of British Columbia. The energy was there, sure enough, but getting the gas to markets was a problem.

The result was Westcoast Transmission Ltd., which he created in 1949. He had persuaded the Social Credit government of B.C. to permit private gas drilling on Crown reserves in 1947 and had bought up the first three drilling permits. Now, after clearing up legal obstacles on both sides of the Canada-U.S. border, Westcoast was able to build a 1127-kilometre gas pipeline 76 centimetres in diameter. McMahon has been given credit for the development of British Columbia's oil and gas industry.

That McMahon luck, backed by analysis and work, clicked in other areas as well. His investments in

Broadway musicals paid off with such blockbusters as *Pajama Game* and *Damn Yankees*. One of his many racehorses, Majestic Prince, won both the Kentucky Derby and the Preakness, two of the jewels in thoroughbred racing's Triple Crown.

Luck was with him as well when he established Alberta Distillers in the 1950s. While the company's first batch of whisky was aging, he convinced his managers that the distillery should also make vodka, which requires no aging. Perhaps he knew, somehow, that within the year a vodka-drinking craze would hit New York and then sweep the continent. Or was it just luck?

Frank McMahon's business successes allowed him to maintain residences in several cities. He retired in Vancouver and then died, in 1986, at another home in Bermuda, yet his name is most noticeable in Calgary. Not Frank McMahon the oilman, of course. Not even the racehorse owner or Broadway "angel." But Frank McMahon the backer of the local football team, the Calgary Stampeders. The team's home, McMahon Stadium—compliments of brothers George and Frank—is a Calgary landmark.

1961–

1970

A Changing Harvest...

Resource development continues to
transform the economic structure of Alberta.

New rail lines push north;
the tar sands are tapped;
and an industrial base
begins to develop
in what was
once a farm province.

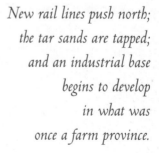

Al Oeming

Albert Frederick Oeming was born in Edmonton but found himself in the South Pacific by his late teens. As a graduate from Strathcona High School during the Second World War, he immediately joined the armed services. Al served in the Pacific with the Royal Canadian Navy Voluntary Reserve. It gave him the opportunity to study the exotic wildlife of Australia, New Zealand and the South Sea Islands. The experience ignited a spark in the young man from Alberta. He returned to take a B.Sc. in zoology from the University of Alberta in 1955.

He was now 30 and his love of nature and wildlife had shaped him into an ardent conservationist. That same year he helped persuade the government to ban the killing of grizzly bears in the Swan Hills region. As a protected zone, it could now be used as a source of valuable information about the vanishing species and perhaps preserve this important animal from extinction.

Oeming was more than just an advocate of conservation. He had a specific dream. In 1957, he bought 208 hectares of land southeast of Edmonton and began to build the Alberta Game Farm. The idea was to build up a comprehensive collection of Canadian animals, especially Canadian hoofed animals, and to acclimatize exotic species that had never before been kept in such winter conditions. The farm opened to the public on August 1, 1959. From modest beginnings it grew to one of the finest ungulate collections in the world.

Oeming, as director of Alberta Game Farm, traded in exotic animals with nations all around the world. He played a major role in pioneering new methods of keeping wild animals successfully in captivity. He was particularly proud of his collection of cheetahs, and toured the country with them and lecturing on conservation.

In 1956, Al was elected a Fellow of the London Zoological Society and in 1969 was awarded the Everly Medal (U.S.A.) for excellence in conservation. He was president of the Edmonton Zoological Society for nine years. In 1972, he received an honorary doctorate of laws from the University of Alberta. He also narrated wildlife films, and in 1971 was featured in an hour-long National Geographic Society TV special *Journey to the High Arctic.*

In the early 1980s, Oeming began to specialize in cold-climate animals. He renamed his game farm Polar Park and continued to operate it for the next decade. By 1996, however, interest had tapered off to the point where it was no longer feasible to keep it open.

Now in his early 80s, Oeming continues to live at the site of his game farm. He has a large collection of farm antiques and horse-drawn vehicles, and has hosted an annual auction every spring since 1989.

Violet Archer

In 1962, the Music Department at the University of Alberta had just four faculty members. The newest was a petite Montreal woman with a giant reputation as a pianist, teacher and composer.

Violet Archer was born in 1913 to Italian-Canadian parents named Balestreri. At 10 she began to take piano lessons. By the time she was 17 she was convinced that music would be her profession. In order to learn composition, she studied all the orchestral instruments and began to write works for orchestra. "Everything I did pointed toward orchestral writing," she said. "I was mesmerized by the orchestra."

She enrolled in the music program at McGill University, where she received a Bachelor of Music degree in 1936. Twelve years later she was granted a Master's degree from Yale University. In the meantime, she had studied under the Hungarian composer Bela Bartok and the American Paul Hindemith. She also made her Montreal debut as a composer-pianist in 1942.

She did not restrict her composition to orchestral work. She wrote choral and chamber pieces as well as songs. She even composed a comic opera, *Sganarelle*, based on a play by Moliere, that had its debut in 1974 at the U of A. Three years earlier, she had received her doctorate in Music from McGill.

One critic found in her music "…a loftiness of purpose, an economy of means and a mastery of musical media. Violet Archer," he wrote, "has a touch of genius."

Archer wrote for a variety of instrumental combinations, but her first love was writing for solo voice and piano. She described herself as a neo-classicist, but she was considered among Canada's most modern composers. In fact, she gave Alberta's first demonstration of electronic music in 1964.

Of more than 280 compositions, her own favourite was a cantata called *The Bell*, based on John Donne's *Meditation XVII*. When another work of hers called *Psalmody* received its premiere performance in 1979, one critic called the occasion "Dr. Archer's finest hour."

Before coming to
Edmonton as an
associate profes-
sor she had been
composer-in-resi-
dence at North
Texas State Univer-
sity and the Univer-
sity of Oklahoma.
She described the
teacher's responsi-
bility to students
in these terms:
"You must be inter-
ested in them, help
them to unfold."

Archer also felt
that schools have
an obligation to
Canadian com-

posers. "It's imperative for our schools to lead the way in performance
of Canadian music and awareness of it."

Although she retired from the U of A in 1978, Archer maintained her momentum. She became a Member of the Order of
Canada in 1983, and was named Composer of the Year by the
Canadian Music Council in 1984. In 1998, she moved to Ottawa to
be closer to her family, but continued to teach there until weeks
before her death, on February 22, 2000.

As a teacher of musical theory and composition Archer was
always well known for her emphatic opinions. She dismissed one
work by Beethoven as "absolute nonsense" and described compositions by Richard Strauss as "dreadful stuff" and "boring." As a composer, however, she recognized the need for background and discipline. "If you are going to break the rules," she says, "you have to
know them first."

Max Bell

Like many Canadians, George Maxwell Bell had grandparents who were prairie pioneers. His grandfather began his career as a black-smith in the early 1880s, and later became the Minister of Telephones in the second legislature in Saskatchewan. Max's father was a postal clerk who eventually became a western newspaper magnate.

In keeping with the family tradition, Max was to become a pioneer in his own right. Born in Regina in 1912, he graduated from McGill University in Montreal to find Canada's business and industry crippled by the Great Depression. Unable to find work, the commerce graduate went prospecting for gold in the Kootenays. Three hard years of work were reduced to six ounces of gold, which were stolen from him. Max would have returned home empty-handed had he not made money during this time by supplying the CPR with railway ties.

He invested these profits in the Turner Valley oil field—one of the first significant oil finds in Alberta. It proved a very good choice for the one-percent shareholder.

Things took a turn for the worse when his father died in 1936. Max went to Calgary to clear up the estate and discovered that his father's newspaper, *The Albertan*, was in debt to the Royal Bank for half a million dollars. To bail out the paper Max borrowed $35,000 from four friends. Three years later all debts were paid. His taste of success in the Turner Valley venture led him to further investments in the petroleum industry. He formed a company to buy rights on Crown oil reserves.

When he did strike oil, he formed a production company to refine and market it.

Reflecting on the exciting days of the petroleum boom, Bell said that some of his theories then were "hare-brained schemes." But they paid off.

The profits from the oil game allowed him to buy the *Edmonton Bulletin* in 1948. It folded three years later. He then bought controlling shares in three other newspapers. Soon he went into partnership with Victor Sifton, owner of several Canadian dailies. Their company, F.P. Publications Ltd., was soon to have daily newspapers in Calgary, Lethbridge, Winnipeg, Ottawa, Toronto, Vancouver and Victoria.

The holdings of this company made Max a recognized financial wizard. Now he had time to indulge in his hobbies. He was an avid fan of horse racing, so he bought a ranch and 100 racing thoroughbreds. He collected Canadian art, played hockey and was an active and generous member of the Presbyterian Church.

When asked once how he accounted for his success. Max said, "The Lord put me in the right place at the right time with the right friends. I'm happy to say that we all made some money."

Max Bell died in 1972 at the age of 59. He left over $20 million to charitable organizations and bequeathed over $2 million to his family. People who knew this quietly successful man described him as "a reluctant inspiration to all."

Andy Russell

Andy Russell was born in 1915 on a ranch in southern Alberta. He dropped out of school after grade 10 in the Dirty Thirties to earn a living trapping and busting broncos. By the age of 19 he had become a first-class professional mountain guide, the youngest to hold a Grade A rating in the province.

Andy married Anna Kathleen (Kay) Riggall, daughter of the noted guide Bert Riggall. Their honeymoon was a sheep hunt in the

mountains. In 1945, Andy began a writing career with a story in *Outdoor Life*. He took over Riggall's outfit in 1946, renaming it Skyline Pack Train. By the 1960s, it became apparent that the pack train business was being killed by industrial encroachment, so Andy took to cattle ranching.

In 1959, Andy helped organize the first successful expedition to capture Dall sheep in the Yukon. From the film footage of this trip grew the plan for the Grizzly Country project. The idea was that Andy and his sons Dick and Charlie would study and film the life of the grizzly bear in a large area of the most rugged country on the continent. *Grizzly Country*, the film and the book, represent a significant contribution to the world's understanding of grizzlies.

In an eventful life, Andy was a big game hunter, outfitter, guide, trapper, rancher, photographer, filmmaker, storyteller, expert marksman, lecturer and writer. He outfitted and led many successful expeditions, including several to the Arctic. Andy Russell's accomplishments and adventures could fill volumes of the best reading to be found. Despite limited formal schooling, the knowledge of nature he built through years of close, patient observation earned him the respect of naturalists worldwide.

Russell's honours include the Order of Canada (1977), Canadian Outdoorsman of the Year (1979) and the Jerry Potts Award, also in 1979. He was a member of the Explorers Club of New York, an honour that he held in common with Lowell Thomas, John Glenn and Jacques Cousteau. In 2002, the Alberta government awarded him the Order of the Bighorn in recognition for his contribution to fish and wildlife conservation.

Russell captivated readers for decades, writing 13 books, many of them bestsellers. A 14th, *Wild Country: The Best of Andy Russell* was released in 2004. He reached an even wider audience in the 1980s with "Our Alberta Heritage," a decade-long series of historical vignettes for radio.

He continued to live in his log cabin, Hawk's Nest, just outside of Waterton Lakes National Park, until he was well into his 80s. After a series of small strokes, however, he found it difficult to get around in the woods and moved into nearby Pincher Creek in 2002. After suffering a bad fall in 2004, his health deteriorated and he died in June 2005 at the age of 89.

No matter where he hung his hat, he lived every minute of his life to the fullest. In the final chapter of *Wild Country*, he wrote, "the wisdom of the years tells me that getting old is a frame of mind, and the way to stay young is to listen to your dreams and to keep one's vision more ahead than behind."

John Decore

John N. Decore—teacher, lawyer, politician and judge—was not one to tolerate intolerance. When he retired as Chief Judge of the District Court of Alberta in 1979, a colleague said, "Some members of minority groups are tempted sometimes anxiously to seek acceptance; John Decore demanded it as a right." He had Ukrainian ancestry and was proud of it.

He was born in 1909 and took his early schooling in Andrew and Vegreville. During the Depression he taught school to finance the study of law at the University of Alberta. He received his law degree in 1938 and practised in Vegreville, St. Paul and Edmonton.

As a Liberal, John Decore was elected in 1949 to represent Vegreville in the House of Commons. He was re-elected in 1953 but did not run in the 1957 election. In the House, John Decore often advocated the rights of immigrants and minority groups. From Hansard, June 13, 1950: "Too often in the past have we found people prejudiced because of a man's colour, or because of the church he attends, or because of his racial origin, or because his name does not sound Anglo-Saxon."

While in Ottawa he was an advisor to the Secretary of State for External Affairs, Lester B. Pearson. As a member of Canada's delegation to the United Nations, he spoke on various humanitarian issues. During that period his chief, Lester Pearson, received the Nobel Peace Prize. In 1957, John Decore nominated "Mike" Pearson as national leader of the Liberal Party.

In 1957 he also left politics to spend more time with his family. The Decores moved to Edmonton, where John helped establish a chair of Ukrainian Studies at the University of Alberta. He also became the first president of the Ukrainian Professional and Businessmen's Club in 1960.

John Decore was named a Queen's Counsel in 1964. The same year he was appointed Chief Judge of the District Court of Northern

Alberta. During 15 years on the Bench, he was instrumental in amalgamating the northern and southern divisions of that court. This led, in 1979, to the merger of the district court with the Trial Division of the Alberta Supreme Court into a new judicial body, the Court of Queen's Bench.

The man known affectionately by his fellow judges as the "Iron Uke" received an honorary doctorate from the U of A in 1980. He advised graduates not to become "...so self-satisfied that you fail to see that others are less advantaged nor...so self-important or God-like that you exempt yourselves from the certain obligations in our society." In his many careers and in his personal life, John Decore always accepted those obligations.

He died in Edmonton in 1994, at the age of 85.

Grant MacEwan

One of Grant MacEwan's biggest complaints about the world was conformity. "Everyone wants to conform, to be the same as the other fellow." Many might disagree, but no one could ever accuse Grant MacEwan of being ordinary. As a farm boy, student, civil servant, agriculturist, author, lecturer, show-ring judge, politician and public servant, he never allowed himself to follow the beaten path.

Grant's parents were pioneers, not once but twice. They were from Nova Scotia, where Grant was born in 1902. When he was six, the family moved and settled north of Brandon, Manitoba, to do mixed farming, "…the most important day of my life," he later said. And he was right. Once in Brandon, Grant entered two worlds— the world of the successful student who played hockey and baseball, and the world of business. By the time he was 12, he had discovered many ways of earning a dollar, from selling newspapers to running the local grocery store.

Seven years later, property values in Brandon crashed and so did the family fortunes. It was time to become pioneers again and they moved west to Melfort, Sakatchewan. Grant was 13 and was expected to do a man's work, helping to turn a patch of bald prairie into a farm.

Six years later, Grant went to agricultural college and embarked on a 23-year-long career as professor and dean of agriculture at the universities of Saskatchewan and Manitoba. He soon earned an international reputation as an agricultural advisor and writer of western Canadian history. He also met and married a schoolteacher named Phyllis Cline. Early in their marriage, he warned her that he didn't plan to spend his life gathering moss while collecting a university professor's pension. He was true to his word.

In 1951, he got an unexpected opportunity to run as the Liberal candidate in a federal by-election in Brandon. Grant was thoroughly beaten, but he was later glad he had lost. Winning would have meant leaving his beloved West for Ottawa. His next opportunity to enter politics was at the civic level, and he became an alderman in Calgary from 1953 to 1958. He went on to become leader of the Alberta Liberal party in 1959, and was mayor of Calgary from 1963 to 1965.

He became lieutenant-governor of Alberta in 1966. During the next eight and a half years, he transformed the office, reaching out to Albertans with his warm, down-to-earth personal style. He became the province's all-time most beloved lieutenant-governor, a distinction he didn't have to share until Lois Hole was appointed in 1999.

He received countless awards in his lifetime, including an Office of the Order of Canada, and a membership in the Alberta Order of Excellence. However, no tribute pleased him more than the one he received in 1971, when Edmonton's new community college was named in his honour.

In his later years MacEwan maintained his remarkable pace as an author, releasing an average of one new history book every year. He continued an active and visible presence in his province almost up until his death at the age of 97, on June 15, 2000. Less than two weeks after his passing, the province announced the creation of an annual $25,000 literary award in his name.

Roland Michener

The third governor general of Canada born in this country was born in 1900 in Lacombe. Daniel Roland Michener seemed destined for state-craft. His father led Alberta's Conservative Party for 10 years and later became a senator. Just after "Roly" was born, the family moved to Red Deer, where he was remembered as "a nice little boy with wavy hair."

In high school he owned a pair of cows. Their milk supplied the family and also provided money to help further his education. His studies at the University of Alberta were briefly interrupted in 1918 for service in the First World War. When he graduated in 1920, he received both the Governor General's Medal for top student and a Rhodes Scholarship to study law in England.

At Oxford University he excelled in sports, especially track and hockey. One hockey teammate was Lester B. Pearson, who later became prime minister of Canada. Although they supported different political parties, Roly and Pearson became close friends. They were partners in the Canadian Open Tennis Tournament one year, but lost in the first round.

After Oxford, Roland Michener returned to Canada and set up a successful law practice in Toronto. In 1945, he was elected to the Ontario legislature and served as provincial secretary until he lost his seat in 1948. Five years later he became a Member of Parliament. With the Conservatives in power in 1957, he was elected Speaker of the House of Commons. He held that post until his defeat in the 1962 election.

Early in his career Roland Michener explained his political philosophy: "My special approach to politics is the legal rights of the people and constitutional safeguards and guarantees. I think there is a fundamental contribution to be made in guaranteeing these rights."

In 1963, he chaired a royal commission on local government in Manitoba. The next year his old friend Lester Pearson named him Canada's High Commissioner to India. The man he succeeded, Chester Ronning, was also an Albertan.

In the Commons and abroad, Roland Michener had a reputation for dignity and fairness. He learned to speak both French and Hindi. And he was always impeccably dressed. In India he was one of the few diplomats to wear a suit and vest in even the hottest weather.

When Governor General Georges Vanier died in 1967, Prime Minister Pearson again turned to his friend. One of Michener's early acts was the creation of an Honours Secretariat to oversee the newly instituted Order of Canada. Roland and Norah Michener presided at Rideau Hall until 1974. It was a period noted for warm and gracious hospitality.

Michener was probably the most physically fit governor general in Canadian history. Even in his 70s, his wavy hair and trim moustache a snowy white, he could be seen jogging briskly on the Rideau Hall grounds.

After leaving Rideau Hall, Michener was elected Chancellor of Queen's University, a position he held until retiring in 1980. In 1979 Premier Peter Lougheed announced the naming of "Mount Michener," which can be seen from Highway 11. On Canada Day, 1982, at the age of 82, Michener celebrated by climbing the peak.

In his last years, he spent much of his time promoting physical fitness, even appearing in Participaction television commercials. "I'm as old as the century," he joked, "but I can withstand a lot." Sure enough, he remained active until shortly before his death in 1991, at the ripe old age of 91.

Ernest Manning

Ernest Manning was a tough-minded administrator and a deft politician who ruled longer than any other provincial premier in Canadian history.

Ernest Charles Manning grew up on a farm in Rosetown, Saskatchewan. One Sunday morning he heard a radio broadcast that changed his life and the life of Alberta. The speaker was William Aberhart, a Calgary school principal and fundamentalist preacher. Ernest Manning was spellbound. When Aberhart announced that he was establishing a school called the Prophetic Bible Institute, the young Manning packed his bags and became the first student to enrol. He lived in the Aberhart home and became an ardent disciple of "Bible Bill."

After graduation, Ernest became a lecturer at the institute and Aberhart's right-hand man. He shared Aberhart's conversion to the

Social Credit money theory as the answer to the Great Depression. When Aberhart became premier in 1935, Ernest Manning became a Cabinet minister— Canada's youngest at the age of 26.

William Aberhart died in 1943, and the Social Credit caucus unanimously chose Manning to succeed him. There were predictions that the end was near for Social Credit, but Manning led the party to victory after victory, often with overwhelming majorities. And he presided for 25 of the most dynamic years of Alberta's history, as the province moved from a quiet farm-based economy to a bustling centre of the energy industry.

He also took over the radio evangelism of Aberhart. His program, *Canada's*

National Back to the Bible Hour, boasted a half-million weekly listeners across Canada. He didn't mix his political philosophy into the religious message as Aberhart had blatantly done. Still, the weekly exposure undoubtedly helped secure his political base.

Religion, politics and farming formed the trinity of Ernest Manning's life. He owned a dairy farm just outside Edmonton. From time to time there were hints of scandal within his government, but his personal integrity was never challenged. Neither was the sincerity of his religious beliefs. "Religion isn't something you keep on a shelf and only take down on a Sunday," he often said.

Ernest Manning held several Cabinet portfolios himself, and although he demanded high performance from his other ministers, he listened to their opinions, saying, "You can't learn anything when you're talking."

In 1968, Manning retired as premier. The year before he had written a book called *Political Realignment: a Challenge to Thoughtful Canadians*. It suggested that a new grouping of "social conservative" forces was needed in Canadian politics. At the same time, he admitted that he thought Social Credit was dead as a political force at the federal level. Many members of his party felt betrayed. The feeling grew after he retired to start a consulting firm. He accepted positions on the boards of several companies, including a bank. Social Credit had based much of its early program on opposition to the Canadian chartered banks.

Prime Minister Pierre Trudeau appointed Manning to the Senate of Canada in 1970, making him the first Social Credit member to be appointed to the Red Chamber. Manning served in the Senate for the next 13 years, until 1983. Two years earlier, the Province of Alberta had made him the first inductee to its Order of Excellence.

Manning spent his final years largely out of the public eye, though he did emerge occasionally to speak in support of the Reform Party of Canada, led by his son Preston. He passed away February 16, 1996, at the age of 87.

Mel Hurtig

He might have become a furrier. For three years after high school he did work in his family's fur store in Edmonton—"...one of the most boring things I have ever done in my life." Fortunately—for Hurtig and for Canada—boredom hasn't been a recurring theme in his life. Since walking out on the fur business more than 50 years ago, he has been a busy man indeed.

Hurtig first made his mark as a bookseller, opening a store in 1956. "I had so little money and so few books that I turned them face outwards to make the shelves look full," he says. Hurtig's Books quickly became a fixture in downtown Edmonton, offering patrons couches and coffee long before they became common in bookstores. Hurtig eventually expanded to three locations, with total annual sales topping $700,000.

Hurtig sold his stores in 1972 because, in his words, "Instead of being a bookseller, I had become an accountant." In the meantime,

Hurtig had dipped a fateful toe into the realm of publishing. He launched Hurtig Publishers Ltd. in 1967, with $30,000 of borrowed money, and published a total of seven titles in his first year. When one of those books won the Governor General's Award for poetry, Mel Hurtig, publisher, became an important person in Canadian literary circles. Over the next 34 years, Hurtig published scores of Canadian bestsellers—all without leaving his native Edmonton.

By 1980, Hurtig had spent years trying to raise funds for his dream project: an affordable Canadian encyclopedia. Finally, in desperation, he approached Premier Peter Lougheed. Lougheed stunned him by offering to fund the project in its entirety, and to donate a copy to every library and school in Canada.

The three-volume first edition, launched in September 1985, quickly became a sensation. It sold out within months, gathering ecstatic press from coast to coast. One reviewer called it "the intellectual equivalent of the building of the CPR." In retrospect, it was. Now available for free on the Internet, the Canadian Encyclopedia is more accessible and affordable than its creator ever dreamed.

As a passionate, outspoken Canadian, Hurtig has always found time for political involvement. In 1970, he helped found the Committee for an Independent Canada, for which he later served as national chairman. He was an early supporter of Pierre Trudeau and ran unsuccessfully as a Liberal candidate in the 1972 federal election. The next year, however, he left the party because of differences over the issue of foreign ownership. During the campaign, Prime Minister Trudeau had described Hurtig as a thorn in his side.

In 1985 Hurtig was founding chairman of the Council of Canadians, an organization devoted to preserving Canada's economic independence. In 1991, he released his first book, *The Betrayal of Canada*. It became the year's best-selling Canadian title.

The following year, he formed the National Party of Canada and led a slate of 171 candidates in the 1993 federal election. However, the party failed to elect any candidates. The following year, it was disbanded after a dispute between Hurtig and Bill Loewen, the party's main financial backer. Hurtig has called the episode "the biggest setback of my life."

He's no longer a bookseller, a publisher or a politician, but Hurtig still manages to stay busy. He has published four best-selling books in the past ten years—all (naturally) focusing on issues of Canadian identity. Above all, he remains as vocal as ever; no article or column on Canadian independence would be complete without a quote from Mel Hurtig.

1971—

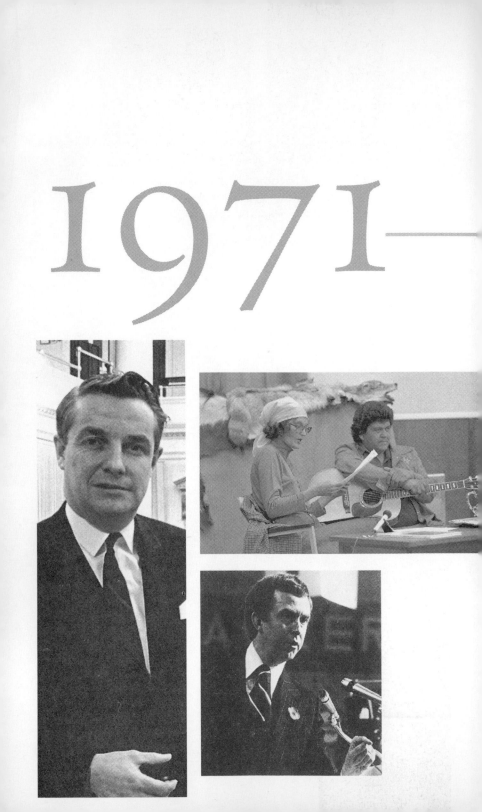

1980

...So Shall They Reap

*A new confidence emerged in the social,
cultural and economic life of Alberta.*

*The province became a consistent
challenger in arts, sports and politics
as prosperity continued
to fuel its rapid expansion.*

*Abundance brought fresh
responsibilities and problems.*

Peter Lougheed

Whenever Albertans have rejected a government, they have done it decisively. Monday, August 30, 1971 was no exception. That morning Peter Lougheed set the barometer in his Calgary home to "change" before going to vote. Change came quickly. By evening, Alberta voters had approved Daylight Saving Time, and they had made Peter Lougheed, 43, their new premier.

The sudden change toward Lougheed's Progressive Conservatives had been six years in the making. When he became leader in 1965, the party had no members in the Alberta legislature. Now it had 49. Social Credit, which had formed the government for 36 years, was reduced to 25 seats.

No one who had known Peter Lougheed for long was surprised that he could achieve such a feat. His reputation as an organizer stretched back to Calgary's Central High School, where he started the first student council.

Edgar Peter Lougheed was born in 1928 into one of Calgary's leading families. His grandfather, Sir James Lougheed, had been Alberta's first senator. His maternal great-grandmother was Métis. Another branch of the Lougheed family, spelling its name differently, had established the giant Lockheed aircraft corporation in California.

Like many other prairie families, the Lougheeds were hit hard by the Depression. Lougheed's father lost the family home in 1938 for failure to pay taxes (Lougheed House was named a national historic site in 1995, and has recently been restored). As a corporate lawyer and senior executive of the Mannix Corporation, Peter did much to restore the family's position before turning his attentions to politics.

While studying law at the University of Alberta, he excelled at football. They called him the "swivel-hipped half." Later he played professionally with the Edmonton Eskimos for two seasons.

From the U of A he went to Harvard for a Master's degree in Business Administration. A summer training job with Gulf Oil took him to Tulsa, Oklahoma. There he witnessed the effects caused by the end of an oil boom, and he was determined to do what he could to prevent the same thing happening in Alberta.

After August 30, 1971, he had the opportunity to try. World prices for oil and gas began to soar and drilling activity increased in Alberta—along with revenues to the provincial government. This gave Peter Lougheed the political muscle to make some demands on the federal government. His minimum terms: a greater voice for Alberta in national energy policy and observer status at oil and gas trade negotiations.

"If Alberta poker chips are involved at the poker table," he said shortly after becoming premier, "we will be at that table."

Later his government established the Heritage Savings Trust Fund to set aside a portion of provincial oil and gas revenues for the future. It quickly became one of the largest investment funds in the world and has lent money to several other Canadian provinces.

The Progressive Conservatives were re-elected with overwhelming majorities in both 1975 and 1979. Before the 1979 election, Peter Lougheed suggested that it would be his last as party leader. Nevertheless, he continued waging his battle for provincial rights in resource matters with renewed vigour.

Lougheed also championed cultural policy, often at the urging of his wife, Jeanne. When Lougheed turned 70, Fil Fraser said, "I will always remember him as the person who was responsible for the golden age of the arts in Alberta from the '70s up until the mid-'80s."

In 1985, Lougheed retired from public life to practise law in Calgary. Honours quickly followed; in 1986, Peter Lougheed Provincial Park was named, and in 1987 he was made a Companion of the Order of Canada.

He has maintained a prominent presence on the national business scene, and served as a board member for some of Canada's biggest corporations. From 1996 to 2002, he was chancellor of Queen's University in Kingston, Ontario. He continues to practise law as a senior partner in the prestigious firm of Bennett Jones.

Max Ward

From northern bush pilot to head of one of the world's largest charter airlines—that was the flight plan followed by Maxwell William Ward, son of a CNR ticket agent from Edmonton.

Max Ward began flying with the Royal Canadian Air Force in 1940, and for much of the Second World War served as flight instructor at various Canadian air bases. When the war ended, he started flying commercially into the Northwest Territories.

In 1946, he took $4000 that he had saved and borrowed to make a down payment on a three-passenger de Havilland Fox Moth. He now headed his own company, Polaris Charter Ltd. But the Air Transport Board saw the little biplane as inadequate for a charter company and refused Polaris a licence. Max teamed up with another company, Yellowknife Airways Ltd. It soon went sour and he lost both his plane and his money.

Discouraged and broke, he moved to Lethbridge and joined his father-in-law in the construction business. By 1953, however, Max Ward was back in the flying business with a 14-seat de Havilland Otter and a fully licensed company called Wardair.

That company did take off. By 1956, Wardair had 13 employees and was in a position to buy a full-bellied Bristol freighter. Instead of prospectors and medical teams, Max Ward was now able to fly livestock, construction equipment and even pre-fabricated buildings into a rapidly developing North. In 1961, Wardair acquired a four-engine Douglas DC-6AB for $1.5 million. It was ideal for flying cargo into the Arctic when lakes were frozen solid. In the summer months it would be useless for that purpose, so Max decided to convert his new freighter into a passenger carrier. During 1962 it made eight trips over the North Pole to England, Denmark and Norway. Those European trips took 19 hours, plus a one-hour refuelling stop in Greenland.

But the charter-flight concept seemed premature for western Canada. Traffic was lighter than Max Ward expected and the company lost $370,000. "We learned what overseas charters were about," he said, "the hard way." In spite of his second major setback. Ward kept trying. He still had several bush planes operating into the North. By 1965, the charter business was on a solid footing. By 1969, he had added a Boeing 727 and two 707s to his fleet. The signal that he had really arrived, however, was his purchase of a $25 million Boeing 747 in 1973.

Eventually, Max Ward built Wardair into an international chartering giant, with offices in several countries and an annual budget well over $100 million. After the industry was deregulated in 1987, though, the company found itself in a financial crunch. Reluctantly, Ward sold his airline to Pacific Western for $250 million.

He received many honours, including membership in the Order of Canada, the Canadian Aviation Hall of Fame and the Order of Icarus. He won both the Billy Mitchell Award and the McKee

Trophy for his contributions to air transportation. In 1989, he was inducted into Alberta's Order of Excellence.

Ward continued to fly his own Twin Otter (painted in Wardair colours, naturally) until recently. In 2002, at the age of 80, he finally decided it was time to let someone else do the flying.

Ward, who still lives in Edmonton with his wife, Marjorie, once summed up his life's philosophy: "About the only thing that really made me furious was to be told I couldn't do something. As soon as someone said, 'Oh, you could never do that,' I wanted to do it."

Maria Campbell

An autobiography by an Edmonton Métis activist, published in 1973, seared the consciences of many Canadians and inspired a new generation of aboriginal authors. The book was *Halfbreed*, by Maria Campbell.

In eloquently direct prose, Cambell describes the joys and crushing sorrows of growing up a "halfbreed" in northwestern Canada. Without bitterness she tells of raising, then losing, her orphaned brothers and sisters in northern Saskatchewan, of marrying for convenience at the

age of 15, and falling into a life of prostitution, alcoholism and drug addiction on the West Coast.

Halfbreed weaves a shatteringly personal story, but it also reveals a much wider picture of aboriginal suffering, pride and resilience. In the 1970s, a time of political awakening for many Métis and First Nations people, the book served as a rallying cry. It also gave young First Nations writers faith that their voices could finally be heard, and that their trials could be overcome.

Maria Campbell was born in northern Saskatchewan in 1940. Her father was an illiterate trapper. Her mother died when Maria was still in school, leaving her to bring up seven younger brothers and sisters. Fortunately, her convent-educated mother had left her daughter with a love of literature and art.

Then there was Maria's great-grandmother, Cheechum, a powerful woman who lived to 104 and died after being thrown from a runaway wagon. Cheechum was probably the strongest positive influence on Maria's life. She instilled in her great-granddaughter a pride in her mixed-culture heritage, an awareness of the mystic side of life and a commitment to honesty and integrity.

In 1963, after a painful battle with drugs and alcohol, Maria Campbell moved from Vancouver to Edmonton and became active in the human rights movement. She involved herself in the struggles of women prisoners, battered wives and First Nations people. And she decided to tell the "halfbreed" story.

As a writer she has gone on to produce numerous plays for both radio and the live theatre. Her 1986 play *Jessica*, written in collaboration with Linda Griffiths, won Toronto's coveted Dora Mavor Moore Award for Outstanding New Play. She also produced two film scripts for the National Film Board—*The Red Dress* and *Delivery*.

In 1979, Maria Campbell was appointed writer-in-residence at the University of Alberta for one year. She described the position as "like welfare for writers. They give you a pen and paper, telephone and office. I'm even on the dental plan this year!"

The honours continue to roll in for Campbell, who now teaches at the University of Saskatchewan. In 2001, she was granted an

Honorary Doctorate from Athabasca University. In 2004, the jury for the $50,000 Canada Council for the Arts Molson Prize stated, "For her contribution to Canadian and aboriginal literature and significant impact on the cultural evolution of Canada, the jury was unanimous in its choice of Maria Campbell..."

Campbell, herself a grandmother now, still remembers the lessons of fair-mindedness and optimism passed down by Cheechum. She has come to embody the spirit she wrote about near the close of *Halfbreed:* "I believe that one day, very soon, people will set aside their differences and come together as one. Maybe not because we love one another, but because we need each other to survive."

Joseph H. Shoctor

The name "Citadel Theatre" and the name "Joe Shoctor" are frequently mentioned in the same breath. Without Shoctor, there would be no Citadel. In fact, it could be argued that the entire province's reputation for theatrical excellence can be traced back to this one bold, gregarious, outrageous showman.

The Edmonton-born lawyer, fundraiser and drama producer was the son of a peddler and scrap dealer who emigrated from Russia in 1913. At 12 Joe discovered drama and pursued his interest throughout high school. At the University of Alberta he continued this interest (and played football for the Golden Bears). In 1948, he helped revive the Edmonton Eskimos Football Club after 10 years of inactivity.

In the 1960s, his dramatic talents took him to New York, where he produced five plays on and off Broadway. When a woman asked why he wasn't producing plays in Edmonton, he took her question seriously. The idea of the Citadel was born.

Shoctor talked three friends into helping him come up with $100,000 to purchase the Edmonton Salvation Army Citadel, a crumbling old brick structure on 102 Street. The Citadel Theatre's first performance, in November 1965, attracted an audience of 300, and

Shoctor was away to the races. In less than a decade, he was already hatching plans for a spectacular new home for his beloved pet project.

Shoctor became campaign manager for a $6.6 million complex, built on the old market place where Joe's father once ran a stall. Its largest performance space was fittingly named the Shoctor Theatre. A new wing, including the Lee Pavilion and the Maclab Theatre, was added in 1984.

"Theatre adds a dimension to the lives of people," said Joe. "They grow with it, sharing the glory and defeat of the distilled lives that are portrayed on the stage. Theatre enlarges the spirit, just as sports creates heroes. People live more; that's what it's all about. That's why I do it."

Shoctor continued to practise law in Edmonton until 2000, when he retired after 53 years at the bar. In 1999, the stretch of 101A Avenue that borders the Citadel Theatre was renamed Shoctor Alley.

Shoctor died in April 2001 after a sudden heart attack. At the funeral, Mel Hurtig paid tribute to "a man of great vision, great foresight and a dreamer whose dreams came true."

John P. Gallagher

"As smooth in manner as a kitten's wrist." That's how a *Maclean's* magazine writer described John Patrick Gallagher, founder and chairman of Dome Petroleum Ltd. "The celebrated tongue is as silver as the hair." Writer Peter C. Newman described Smilin' Jack's legendary grin as having "a life of its own. Like an Elvis Presley hip wiggle or a Farrah Fawcett hair toss."

Jack Gallagher , born in Winnipeg in 1916, was considered one of the shrewdest men in the Canadian oil patch, a lone wolf who followed his own advice. He often went against the conventional wisdom of the industry he worked in. His petroleum empire ultimately came crashing down around him, but only after one of the greatest runs in Canadian corporate history.

Gallagher studied geology at the University of Manitoba. He discovered the challenge of the North in the 1930s when he was a student working summers for $2.50 a day with the Canadian Geological Survey. He never lost sight of the dream to capture the oil and gas riches of that region.

After graduation Gallagher embarked on a brilliant career with Standard Oil. He worked in 12 foreign countries, mostly in the Middle East and Latin America. In 1950, he was faced with the decision of moving toward Standard's head office or striking out on his own. A group of American investors asked his help to buy into Canadian energy resources, and the decision was easy for Jack Gallagher. He became an independent explorer—a wildcatter.

Dome Petroleum, the company he started, went on to become one of the giants of the Canadian oil business, with assets of more than $8 billion. Gallagher was never considered by his colleagues—or by himself—to be an outstanding geologist. His gift lay in his ability to put together complicated business deals involving other people's money.

Although Dome had some promising oil and natural gas strikes in Alberta, Gallagher's vision was cast much farther north, to the Beaufort Sea. He felt sure that Canada's energy future lay in the far north, and his private—and government—investors were eager to follow the quest. Despite a few major finds, however, the envisaged bonanza never materialized. The company's debt load eventually became too much to bear. When Dome collapsed in 1982, Gallagher resigned, absorbing an estimated personal loss of more than $118 million. Gallagher, always an economic nationalist, found himself a horrified onlooker when the company was sold to American giant Amoco in 1988.

Gallagher went on to other ventures and a contented life, but never recaptured the magic of his glory days. He died in Calgary in 1998 at the age of 82.

The philosophy of "Smiling Jack" Gallagher was simple: "You only go through life once. And it's a lot more fun if you plough a different furrow, rather than the same furrow that everybody else has ploughed."

Ralph Steinhauer

The first Canadian aboriginal to serve as a lieutenant-governor was born on Alberta's Morley Reserve in 1905. Ralph Garvin Steinhauer's family name came from his great-grandfather, the first aboriginal person ordained as a Wesleyan minister. The elder Steinhauer had adopted the name at the request of an American who had provided for his education.

Ralph's aboriginal name, Omsokistikkeeweepow, means "big farmer." True to the name, he spent most of his life farming at Saddle Lake, about 200 kilometres northeast of Edmonton. Ralph spent 37 years as chief and councillor of the Saddle Lake reserve. In 1963, he became the first aboriginal person ever to run for the Liberal party in a federal election. Eleven years later he was appointed Alberta's 10th lieutenant-governor. He served in that capacity until 1979.

Steinhauer had always been active in aboriginal and agricultural organizations. He was founder, director and executive officer of the Alberta Federation of Indians and a board member of the Indian-Eskimo Association. He was president of the Alberta Indian Corporation, and worked with organizations for aboriginal and rural economic development. He was district president of the National

Farmer's Union and was involved with Alberta Newstart and the Northern Development Council.

While Steinhauer was lieutenant-governor, he was the first person from another tribe to be made an honorary chief of the Blood First Nation in southern Alberta. The headdress of eagle feathers was placed on his head, and he received the title Chief Flying Eagle.

Ralph Steinhauer's accolades include a Medal of Service of the Order of Canada. He was made an officer of the Order in 1972. After his term as lieutenant-governor, Steinhauer returned to his farm at the Saddle Lake. He died in Edmonton in 1987, aged 82.

Tommy Banks

Since his appointment to Canada's Senate in April 2000, Albertans have been entitled to refer to him as the Honourable Thomas Banks. But for decades he was simply Tommy Banks, Edmonton's "Mr. Music."

An internationally esteemed producer, pianist, composer, bandleader and arranger, Tommy Banks has been involved in almost every facet of Canadian music-making. As *Maclean's* magazine once remarked, "It might be easier to list the things he doesn't do."

Born in Calgary on December 17, 1936, Banks knew by age five that he would grow up to be a musician. His father was a well-known local musician, his mother was a stage performer, and there was always music playing in the house. The family moved north in 1949; Tommy Banks has since been called "the best gift Calgary ever gave to Edmonton."

His professional career began in 1952, at the tender age of 15, when he quit school to travel with the Jammin' The Blues concert tour. By 17, he was musical director of the Orion Musical Theatre in Edmonton.

For years, Banks was best known for his work in television. In 1968, *The Tommy Banks Show* started a six-year run nationally on CBC TV. As pianist, composer, bandleader and host, he was Johnny Carson and Doc Severinsen rolled into one. Later, at CITV Edmonton, he co-ordinated (and occasionally conducted) the internationally syndicated *Celebrity Concert* series, which paired the Edmonton Symphony with such performers as Aretha Franklin, Engelbert Humperdinck and Tom Jones.

He ranks among Canada's most renowned jazz pianists, whether playing solo, with a quartet or in front of a band. A highlight came in 1978, when his big band (which at the time included such great Alberta musicians as Clarence "Big" Miller and P.J. Perry) played at Sweden's Montreaux Jazz Festival. The double album recorded at that concert went on to win a Juno Award and the Grand Prix du Disque as the year's best jazz recording (it has since been reissued on CD).

He has been front and centre at some of Canada's biggest events, serving as music director for Edmonton's Commonwealth Games in 1978 and Universiade in 1983, at Vancouver's Expo '86 and at the 1988 Winter Olympics in Calgary.

For decades, nearly every emerging Albertan musician has been supported or promoted in some way by Banks. In 1978, he was the founding chair of the Alberta Foundation for the Performing Arts, the province's main performance funding body. He remained in the position until 1986. From 1983 to 1987, he chaired the music program at Edmonton's Grant MacEwan College. Throughout, he was always ready to offer advice or encouragement to young Albertan performers. After hiring one young band for an event in 1988 (paying the group's

asking price), he told them sternly, "Never work for so little again."

Banks served for six years as a member of the Canada Council, and was made an Officer of the Order of Canada in 1991. He was inducted into the Alberta Order of Excellence in 1993. In June 1999, Edmonton gave the street that fronts the Edmonton Jazz Society a fitting new name: Tommy Banks Way.

Banks' life changed gears abruptly in 2000 when, out of the blue, Jean Chrétien phoned to ask if he would accept a posting to the Senate. Although new to politics, he soon established himself as a respected voice in Ottawa. He now divides his time between Ottawa and Edmonton, which is home to his wife Ida and their three grown children.

Don Smith

William Donald Smith was born with a knack for fostering talent in others. He took Alberta from a province with few top-calibre swimmers in the 1960s to one of the strongest forces in the country.

The future member of the Alberta Sports Hall of Fame was born in 1921 in Port Colbourne, Ontario. He began teaching and coaching aquatics 25 years later, and became one of the country's most inspirational swimming coaches and sports educators.

In 1947, Don joined the University of Alberta physical education staff. He received his doctorate in education from the University of

Buffalo in 1957. Smith held many executive positions in swimming associations throughout his career. One of the most outstanding was as team manager of the National Swimming Championships, involving the Canadian Olympic swimming and diving team at Mexico City in 1968. Another such outstanding responsibility was his work as chairman of the national swim team from 1967 to 1970. In 1970, he went to the Commonwealth Games in Edinburgh as assistant coach.

Smith acted as official representative of the Canadian Amateur Swimming Association to both the Canadian Olympic Association and the Canadian Pan American Games Association.

For seven years, Dr. Smith was a volunteer leader of the Boy Scouts and Wolf Cubs. He was the national president of the Canadian Association for Health, Physical Education and Recreation from 1967 to 1969.

The responsibilities Don Smith assumed in the world of sports go on and on. In recognition of his many achievements he was made a Fellow of the American College of Sports Medicine. He also received the Badge of Service and was given an honorary membership in the Canadian Red Cross Society. In 1974, he was inducted into the Alberta Sports Hall of Fame, along with his daughter, Becky, inducted for her Olympic successes in 1976 in Montreal.

His practice, as aquatic coach, was to get the masses swimming and then skim the cream off the top for international competition. His philosophy for the individual was "always finish what you start, and be ready to suffer hard times without pity."

Don saw a life's dream fulfilled in 1976 when two of his eight children, Becky and Graham, won medals at the Montreal Olympic Games. Shortly after, on September 1, 1976, he died of cancer.

Joe Clark

Canada's youngest-ever prime minister was also the first born in the West. Charles Joseph Clark came from the foothills town of High River. He was sworn into office on June 4, 1979, the day before he turned 40.

Both Clark's father and grandfather had been editors of the *High River Times*. His own early ambition was to become a famous sportswriter, but by the time he was 17, he had been bitten by the political bug. It happened when he on a scholarship visit to Ottawa. The House of Commons was in an uproar over the Liberals' use of closure to end debate on the proposed trans-Canada natural gas pipeline, and

Clark was fascinated by the drama. Not long afterward, the newly elected John Diefenbaker visited High River. Joe Clark met him and decided that, like Diefenbaker, he would be prime minister some day.

As a boy, Joe was considered a loner, more interested in books than in games. He began to blossom while studying history at the University of Alberta. He edited the student newspaper, *The Gateway*, developed a reputation as a campus prankster and plunged seriously into politics.

After Peter Lougheed became leader of Alberta's Progressive Conservatives, Joe was hired as the party's provincial organizer. But a backroom role wasn't enough for him. In 1967, he ran as a provincial candidate in Calgary South, considered a rock-solid bastion of the ruling Social Credit Party. He surprised everyone except himself by coming within 461 votes of winning.

In 1970, after polishing his French on a tour of Europe, Joe returned to Alberta to teach political science and complete his MA. Two years later he was elected as Member of Parliament for Rocky Mountain in western Alberta. The job brought him together with a headstrong young Ottawa political worker, Maureen McTeer, and the two were married in 1973.

When Robert Stanfield resigned in 1976, Clark decided to take a run at the leadership, although it was clearly a two-candidate race between Brian Mulroney and Claude Wagner. When the smoke had cleared, the 37-year-old "Joe Who?" had sneaked up the middle to become the new national leader of the Progressive Conservatives.

Three years later he was elected prime minister in a minority government, breaking an 11-year reign by Pierre Elliott Trudeau. It wasn't a long stay. On December 13, 1979, the budget was defeated in a non-confidence vote. Two months later, Trudeau was back as prime minister.

For much of the next three years, Clark's Conservatives led the Liberals in the polls, but party insiders worried that he would never be able to win an election outright. He decided to put his leadership to the test at a convention, and lost to Brian Mulroney.

After Mulroney was elected prime minister, Clark served as Secretary of State for External Affairs and, later, Minister of Constitutional Affairs. In 1993, exhausted and disappointed by the failed referendum to support the Charlottetown Accord, he retired. After five years of teaching and consulting, however, he returned to the fray. In 1998, he once again became leader of the Progressive Conservatives.

By the time he retired from politics for good, in 2004, Joe Clark had irrefutably earned the stature of statesman. He built a legacy of universal respect, founded on the philosophy he had followed throughout his career. He stated it clearly when he was 27, to a student audience in Red Deer: "Look at your world with your own eyes, and do things that need to be done."

1981—

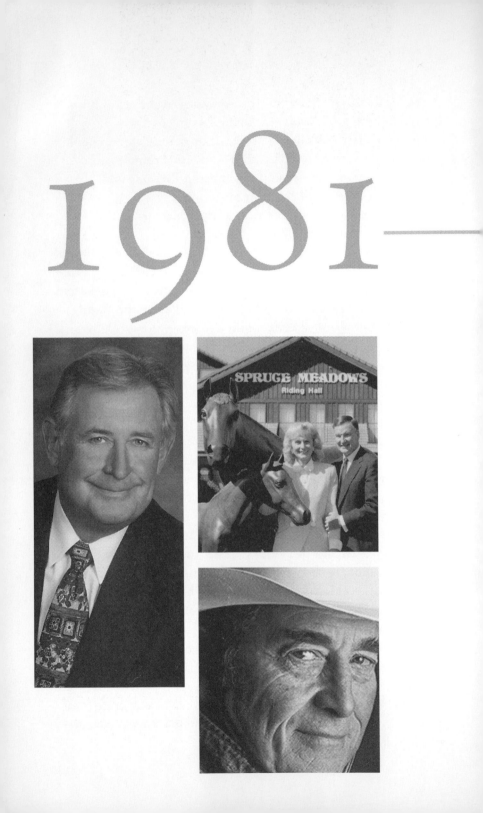

2005

The New Millenium...

In 1980, Alberta was well established as one of the richest provinces in Confederation.
We had big cities and there was lots going on in the arts and culture, industry, research, agriculture, education and tourism.

But the energy crisis, the National Energy Policy and high interest rates caused difficulties throughout the province.

In the 1990s, the province struggled with cutbacks and privatization.

But today, in 2005, oil revenues are again high and the prospect of prosperity is at the gates.

Kurt Browning

One day, a skinny little farm kid from Caroline, Alberta, wandered into a figure skating class, hoping to improve his hockey skills. He ended up becoming the greatest athlete to ever lace up a pair of

skates in Alberta, with the possible exception of Wayne Gretzky.

Kurt Browning was a surprise right from the start. He was born June 18, 1966 to Dewey and Neva Browning who, both in their 40s, thought their diaper-changing days were behind them (Kurt's brother Wade is 11 years older and his sister Dena is nine years older).

The coach at Browning's first figure skating class, Karen McLean, spotted a strong glimmer of potential. Within a year, at age 11, Browning had won his first competition, and by the mid-80s he had emerged as one of Canada's up-and-coming young skaters.

Browning qualified for the 1988 Olympics in Calgary. There, however, the spotlight was on Brian Orser and his much-publicized gold-medal duel with American Brian Boitano. Browning quietly finished eighth overall, achieving his goal of a top-ten finish.

After the Olympics, gold medallist Boitano talked openly about his one remaining career goal: to become the first skater to land a quadruple jump in international competition. Said Orser at the time, "Of course, someone could beat him to the quad." He was talking about Browning.

Sure enough, a month later at the world championships in Budapest, Browning landed the quad, thus securing a permanent place in skating history. His dazzling free skate was enough to lift him to a sixth-place finish—a huge breakthrough for someone who had finished 15th the year before.

At the 1989 championships in Paris, Browning and his coaches optimistically hoped for a bronze medal. Instead, Browning shocked the world by vaulting straight to the top of the podium, nailing yet another quad in the process.

He repeated his championship performance in 1990, in Halifax. Then, in Munich in 1991, he became the first male skater in Canadian history to win the world championships three years in a row. He won for a fourth time two years later in Prague. In 1990 and 1991, he won the Lionel Conacher Award as Canadian male athlete of the year. In 1992, after recovering from a back injury and a poor showing at the Olympics, he won a silver medal at the world championships in Oakland, CA.

Of course, Browning's career hasn't been without its shattering—and well-publicized—disappointments. He went into the 1992 Olympics in Albertville, France as the prohibitive gold-medal favourite. However, he seemed uncharacteristically nervous in the competition, and he was still recovering from a back injury. Ultimately, he skated to a disastrous sixth-place finish. He stumbled again at Lillehammer in 1994, apologizing in tears to a Canadian television audience after a 12th-place finish in the short program. Buoyed by an outpouring of support, he rebounded with a brilliant long program to finish fifth overall.

Now approaching 40, Browning remains at the top of his game, an active and respected fixture on the professional figure skating circuit. In 1996 he married Sonia Rodriguez, a dancer with the National Ballet who has since become the company's prima ballerina. On July 12, 2003, the couple had a son, Gabriel Browning Rodriguez.

If this little Browning grows up to be a success, it should surprise no one.

Bernard Callebaut

If you're Albertan, and you get a shiny, copper-coloured box of chocolates on Valentine's Day, it can mean only one thing: somebody really loves you.

There was a time, not so long ago, when you would have been thrilled with just any old box of chocolates. Today, however, if it's true love, it has to be Callebaut.

Since 1983, Bernard Callebaut has been teaching Albertans to share his passion for fine chocolate. More recently, he has been reaching out to the rest of the world. Although Calgary remains his company's epicentre (with ten stores), Bernard Callebaut now has stores across Canada, in the U.S. and even in Japan.

Callebaut grew up with chocolate flowing through his veins, as a fifth-generation member of a chocolate-making family in the town of Wieze, Belgium. His great-grandfather opened the Callebaut chocolate factory in 1911, and by the time young Bernard came along, the company had become one of Belgium's biggest and most renowned chocolate producers. At its peak, the factory produced nearly 35 million kilograms of bulk chocolate per year.

Callebaut was born in the family house next to the factory and grew up breathing chocolate-scented air. From his bedroom window, he could jump onto the roof of the factory and sneak in. He knew where the reject chocolates were stored, and became famous at school for always having free chocolate.

As a young man he studied electromechanical engineering, expecting to make his career in the factory. But in 1980, after the death of Callebaut's father and uncle, the family decided to sell the factory to industry giant Suchard Toblerone. Suddenly, Callebaut found himself with a sizeable inheritance and no clearly defined path for the future.

Callebaut decided that he wanted to leave Europe and strike out on his own. He spent the next two years exploring the world, look-ing for a new home. On a trip to Canada, he fell in love with the Rockies. He visited Calgary and realized that its cool, dry climate would be perfect for making chocolates. "Moisture and chocolate are enemies," he says. Besides, he contends, "People in cooler climates eat more chocolate."

Callebaut promptly returned to Belgium and began preparing to move. With his inheritance as start-up capital, he opened the first Chocolaterie Bernard Callebaut on 17th Avenue SW. Instead of producing bulk chocolate, as his family had for generations, he decided to specialize in handmade chocolates.

Over time, word of Callebaut's New-World success drifted across the Atlantic, and in 1996 he was invited to be an honoured guest at France's Festival International du Chocolat, the first person from North America to achieve that distinction. Within three years, he had captured the festival's highest award, the "Grand Prix International Artisan Chocolatier."

Callebaut has accomplished every entrepreneur's dream, of being just one step ahead of an emerging trend. Just as our tastes were becoming more refined, Callebaut was there to satisfy them.

"Twenty-five years ago, if you wanted coffee you paid 25 cents for hot brown water," he says. "Now, people have discovered gourmet coffee and special roasts and blends. Chocolate is the same thing. More than ever, people appreciate quality."

Douglas Cardinal

A Douglas Cardinal building seems almost alive with the rhythmic beat of its curvilinear walls and cascading forms. His structures echo the carvings of First Nations spirit masks, the flow of the land and water, the fierce artistic vision of their creator. They are amazing for being made of brick and mortar.

Doug Cardinal is a world-renowned, visionary architect who has combined modern technologies with traditional First Nations sensibilities to craft revolutionary buildings. Cardinal has changed the urban landscape of Alberta, Canada and elsewhere with his distinctive style. There is simply no mistaking a Cardinal creation.

Cardinal was born in Calgary in 1934, the eldest of eight children. Although his father was of Blackfoot heritage, and his mother Métis and German, both parents did little to acknowledge their Native ancestry. The family moved to the Porcupine Hills, where Cardinal's father worked as a forest ranger, guide and trapper. He shared with his son a deep appreciation of nature.

When Doug Cardinal was seven years old, he was sent to a residential school in Red Deer. Treatment at the school was harsh, and Cardinal and his two younger brothers were frequently beaten. His life was made bearable by the friendship of a young teacher, Mrs. Salter, who supplied him with books about art and architecture and encouraged him to draw. The school at St. Joseph's Convent also exposed Cardinal to the art and architecture of the Catholic Church.

At the age of 18, the talented young Cardinal was admitted to the Faculty of Architecture at the University of British Columbia. Unfortunately, it wasn't ready for a First Nations designer from the backwoods of Alberta. Cardinal was told that a successful architect had to come from the right background and that the son of a Native trapper had no chance. Cardinal headed home after a year and a half. He landed a job at a Red Deer architectural firm, and one of the owners later described Cardinal as "the best draftsman and designer I ever employed."

When he was 21, Cardinal broke his back in a car accident. During his recovery, he was forced to focus on how short life could be. Suddenly fired up, he applied to the University of Texas' architectural school and graduated with distinction in 1963. He then travelled through Mexico and Arizona, his first exposure to Native American cultures and the Spanish-Indian architecture of 17th-century Mexico. Both helped shape his sense of architectural design.

Cardinal's first significant architectural commission came in 1964, the beautiful St. Mary's Church in Red Deer. To get the effect he wanted, Cardinal had to come up with innovative construction techniques that would allow curving forms, natural lighting over the altar and lectern, and an imaginative use of brick. The church was completed in 1967 to critical acclaim.

Cardinal's reputation quickly grew, and his curving, soaring structures became part of the landscape of one Alberta community after another. Three of his buildings were completed in 1976: Grande Prairie Regional College, the St. Albert Civic and Cultural Centre and the Alberta Government Services Centre at Ponoka. His Edmonton Space Sciences Centre, now called the Odyssium, was finished in 1983.

That year, Cardinal won the contract to design the Canadian Museum of Civilization in Hull, Quebec. It was his greatest work to date, spanning over a million square feet. Critics hailed the museum as "the very symbol of Canada."

Cardinal won the competition to design the National Museum of the American Indian on the Mall in Washington, DC in 1998. Halfway through development, however, he was fired after his wrangling with the contractor created delays. The museum was completed based on Cardinal's original designs but the architect, furious at being dismissed, called the museum "a forgery" and refused to attend the opening ceremonies.

Douglas Cardinal and his team of associates continue to weave architectural magic out of their offices in Ottawa. Cardinal's trademark style of curving brickwork—organic architecture, he calls it—has influenced a new generation of architects around the world. He has designed well over 100 buildings and communities, throughout North America and from Saudi Arabia to Australia.

As the radical young First Nations architect with long black hair and a red suit, Cardinal used to stick out like a sore thumb in the boardrooms where he did business. Now 70 years old, he looks much more corporate in his dress but still doesn't really fit in, and he likes it that way. According to Cardinal, not fitting in is part of the price that must be paid to be creative.

Harold Cardinal

Harold Cardinal is called by some the father of modern aboriginal politics in Canada. Certainly he shall be remembered by history as the young aboriginal leader who had the gall to accuse a prime minister to his face of attempting to exterminate Canada's aboriginal people.

Cardinal was born January 3, 1945, on the Cree reserve of Sucker Creek in northern Alberta. Articulate and activist, he was elected president of the Indian Association of Alberta at the age of 23. That same year, federal Indian Affairs minister Jean Chretien released a white paper on proposed reforms to the Indian Act. The changes would have abolished Indian status and advocated the assimilation of First Nations peoples into mainstream society.

Cardinal was furious with the white paper and headed for his typewriter, determined to do something about it. The result, released in 1969, was the book *The Unjust Society: the Tragedy of Canada's Indians*. In it Cardinal wrote the now famous lines "Generations of Indians have grown up behind a buckskin curtain of indifference, ignorance and, all too often, plain bigotry. The history of Canada's Indians is a shameful chronicle of the white man's disinterest, his trampling of Indian rights."

The book was an instant best-seller and revolutionized the thinking of many mainstream Canadians about the plight of First Nations peoples. Cardinal followed the book with a direct response to the government's white paper, which he called *The Red Papers*, based on months of communications with aboriginal communities around Alberta.

A year later, Harold Cardinal and other Native leaders met with Prime Minister Trudeau and his Cabinet. Cardinal bluntly accused the federal politicians of attempting cultural genocide with their planned reforms.

Cardinal's writings and oratory played a key role in shifting public opinion in favour of continuing a separate status for First Nations peoples that allowed them to preserve their traditional way of life. The Trudeau government eventually backed down from its white paper. Former Manitoba MLA Elijah Harper says Cardinal demonstrated historic leadership.

"He paved the way. He was such a very young man. Challenging the government. Nobody had done that before. We became part of the new revolution, the fight for our rights as Indian people."

Harold Cardinal's role as a significant leader among First Nations communities did not end with the showdown with Trudeau. Cardinal went on to serve nine terms as president of the Indian Association of Alberta. He spent a brief and controversial period in 1977 as the first Native to work as the regional Director-General of Aboriginal Affairs in Alberta. Cardinal played an important role in the creation of the National Indian Brotherhood, which went on to become the Assembly of First Nations. He was frequently involved in negotiations with Ottawa over the direction of federal Indian policy and was one of the aboriginal leaders to play a role in the patriation of the Constitution and the creation of the Charter of Rights and Freedoms.

Cardinal was a scholar as much as he was an activist and political leader. He was in his 40s when he took up the study of law, completing his law degree at the University of Saskatchewan and teaching there as an assistant professor. He went on to earn his Master's degree at Harvard Law School and was called to the bar in Alberta in

2004. A year later, just before his death in June 2005, Cardinal was awarded his PhD in law from the University of British Columbia.

Cardinal's thesis for his doctorate focused on a subject that had long interested him: the relationship between Cree and State law. Professor Wes Pue of the University of British Columbia was Cardinal's doctoral supervisor. He says Cardinal was uniquely qualified for the thesis.

"Dr. Cardinal invested years in acquiring the learning offered by Cree elders. His life quest produced a lawyer and a scholar who uniquely, deeply, bridges two worlds."

Cardinal always stressed the value of education in the lives of aboriginal people, both to his family and to his community at large. His wife Maisie earned her PhD in education prior to Cardinal's death and all six of the couple's children have at least one university degree. Cardinal's family was by his side as he succumbed to lung cancer at the age of 60, on June 3, 2005.

"I knew Dr. Harold Cardinal long before he completed the triple crown of becoming a 'Doctor, Lawyer, and Indian Chief,'" said Phil Fontaine, national chief of the Assembly of First Nations, in paying homage to Cardinal. "He truly has been an inspirational warrior and leader for First Nations all of his life."

Laurence Decore

If you drive along the southern bluffs overlooking the North Saskatchewan River through Edmonton, you will see signs posted for miles that read "Laurence Decore Look-Out." They were posted in the summer of 2004 as a token of respect for the man who dominated the city's civic politics in the 1980s and who put real fear into the ruling provincial Conservatives in the early 1990s.

Laurence Decore was born Lavrentiy Dikur in June 1940, in Vegreville. Laurence and his two brothers followed in their father John's footsteps and went into law. Laurence was called to the bar in 1964. He also showed a flair for business, acquiring shares in hotels, cable television and other enterprises. He was a millionaire before he was 30.

Laurence Decore then continued to look to his father's example by contemplating politics. Decore was smart and feisty and could, on occasion, strike people as somewhat cool and arrogant. He was an impeccable dresser whose suits reflected a sharp and contemporary sense of style. Everything about Decore said he could be the future.

He ran successfully for a seat on Edmonton city council in the 1974 and 1976 municipal elections. Decore then went after the mayor's chair in 1980 and lost but made the attempt again in 1983 and won by a landslide. He enjoyed an even bigger victory in the 1986 municipal election. During his second term as mayor, Decore spearheaded a tough fiscal policy that resulted in the city wiping out its debt.

During his years as mayor, Decore bumped up against the man who would confound his own aspirations in later years. Ralph Klein was mayor of Calgary and the two had their fun resurrecting and inflaming the old Edmonton-Calgary rivalry. On one occasion, Decore challenged Klein to a race down the luge run at Calgary's Olympic Park. Klein took him up on the challenge and thereby provided the public with the spectacle of two middle-aged men of high office stuffed into jump suits and hurtling down a vertical sheet of ice. Decore won the race.

By 1988, Decore was ready for provincial politics. He used his Edmonton power base to trigger a leadership vote in the Alberta Liberal Party and took control of the party on the first ballot. Premier Don Getty called a snap election soon after and the Liberals lost. Decore, however, won his own seat in Edmonton-Glengarry and was in the legislature.

From then on, Decore was relentless in pounding the Conservatives over fiscal mismanagement. He was so effective that polls taken in the early 1990s showed Decore's Liberals ahead of the Tories. A political upset appeared to be in the offing.

Two significant events then happened. Decore discovered he had cancer and underwent a series of treatments. Second, Ralph Klein won the 1992 Conservative leadership convention. Ever the strategist, Klein adopted Decore's platform of fiscal responsibility and smaller government, taking away the Liberal leader's political leverage. By the time the 1993 provincial election rolled around, Klein had turned the tide and the Conservatives held onto power. They still got a scare, however, with the Liberals winning the largest number of Opposition seats since 1917: 32.

Rank-and-file Liberals were frustrated when they did not win the election. Under pressure, Decore stepped down as leader. He stayed on as an MLA until 1997, when he returned to the private sector.

Throughout his years of public service, Laurence Decore concentrated on deepening and extending multiculturalism as a cornerstone of Canadian society. He was also devoted to the preservation and elevation of Ukrainian culture in Canada. Decore played an important role in getting Ukrainian-English bilingual education programs in Edmonton schools and in creating the Ukrainian Heritage Village. As chairman of the Canadian Consultative Council on Multiculturalism, he played a significant role in ensuring that multiculturalism was enshrined in the Charter of Rights and Freedoms. As he was retiring from political life, Decore served as chair of the Canada-Ukraine Business Initiative, building economic links between the two countries.

Ever the fighter, Decore finally surrendered to his lengthy battle with cancer November 6, 1999. "Laurence was a man who brought great passion and a keen intellect to all he did in public life, qualities especially apparent during debates in the legislature," said Ralph Klein of his long-time political rival. "Whether we were working as allies or as political foes, I always felt that he served his constituents and his community."

Fil Fraser

Growing up as an affluent Black kid in a predominantly white, working-class Montreal neighbourhood, Fil Fraser learned a valuable early lesson in life: "You learned when to fight and when to flee."
Fortunately for Alberta, Fraser grew into a man who didn't have to flee very often. He can always be counted on to hold his own. A pioneering filmmaker, respected broadcaster, journalist and educator and an outspoken champion of human rights, he has left an indelible mark on his adoptive province.

Born in Montreal in 1932, Fraser started his career as a radio broadcaster in Toronto, working for legendary hockey announcer Foster Hewitt. In 1958, at age 26, he moved to Regina, and in 1965 to Edmonton. He quickly became an established presence on Alberta airwaves, and in 1969 became program manager and senior producer at Canada's first educational television station, MEETA (which later became ACCESS).

In the 1970s, he set up his own production company. Although the company began small, Fraser had a galvanizing effect on Alberta's film and television industry. He organized the first Alberta Film Festival in 1974, launching an annual event that survives today as the Alberta Motion Picture Industry Association (AMPIA) Awards.

Then, in the late 1970s, Fraser embarked on a very brief, but hugely influential, foray into feature films. The first movie he produced, 1977's *Why Shoot the Teacher?*, became the year's most commercially successful Canadian film. Fraser followed it up with 1978's *Marie Anne* and 1980's *The Hounds of Notre Dame*.

Together, these three films proved it was possible to tell truly western Canadian stories without going broke or boring people silly.

They helped pave the way for a new generation of Alberta filmmakers, people like Anne Wheeler and Francis Damberger.

In the midst of that success, in 1979, Fraser founded the Banff Television Festival. Over time, it grew into one of the international television industry's most important annual events (Fraser remains its honorary chair).

Fraser's eminence extends well beyond the film and television community. Throughout his life, he has been an outspoken and eloquent advocate for multiculturalism and social justice. In 1989, he began a three-year term as chairman of Alberta's Human Rights Commission. In 1990–91 he toured the country as part of the Citizens' Forum on Canada's Future, better known as the Spicer Commission, and in 1991 he was made a Member of the Order of Canada.

In 1994, he returned to the forefront of Canadian broadcasting, as chairman and CEO of Vision TV. The job took him to Toronto for a few years, but he returned to Edmonton as soon as he retired.

Characteristically, Fraser hasn't used retirement as an excuse for slowing down. In 2003 he published *Alberta's Camelot*, a look back at Alberta's flourishing cultural scene in the Lougheed years (of which Fraser was a central figure) and an open plea for improved public support of arts and culture. That same year, he joined the board of Telefilm Canada. He also serves as an adjunct professor in communications at Athabasca University.

Few Albertans are as widely respected or as widely liked as Fil Fraser. He has built a reputation for success without arrogance, of assertiveness without belligerence. In a 1994 interview he said, "…I'm not a rich man, I've lost more than I've made, raised millions for films and never cheated anyone. I can walk up to anyone and smile and get a smile back. I hope I'll be seen as a self-made man who gave more than he took."

The Ghermezians

The founder of the empire-building Ghermezian family, Jacob, was born in Azerbaijan in 1904, a small, landlocked and arid country bordering Turkey and Armenia. He moved to Iran, where he enjoyed success as a rug merchant, married and had four sons. The Orthodox Jew and his family immigrated to Montreal in the 1960s, in part to escape the rising tide of Islamic fundamentalism in Iran. He established a successful chain of Persian rug stores in Canada.

Jacob created Triple Five Corporation when he was 17. The firm's destiny as the ultimate mega-mall developer didn't blossom until Jacob moved with his wife and four sons to Edmonton and struck it rich in real estate in the late 1970s, amassing the largest private portfolio of land in Alberta. About this time, Jacob passed the business on to his eldest son Eksander, aided by brothers Raphael, Nader and Bahman. Jacob passed away in 2000 at the age of 97 years.

If the Ghermezians have always been extremely protective of their privacy, their aggressive business demeanor and epic sense of scale in real estate development have guaranteed that they are the subjects of much public curiosity and periodic government scrutiny. The family first came to broad attention when it announced it intended to build the world's largest indoor shopping mall on residential land on the western outskirts of Edmonton.

Controversy around the project started with allegations that city councillors had been offered bribes in return for changing the zoning of the land where the mall was to be built. In 1975, an inquiry by Justice William Morrow found that councillors had indeed received gifts, but that these did not technically constitute a bribe and no law had been broken.

Phase One of West Edmonton Mall opened in 1980. When Phase Three was completed in 1985, the complex was the largest shopping centre in the world. Ten years later, the continued ownership of West Edmonton Mall by the Ghermezian family was in doubt. The Alberta Treasury Board filed a lawsuit, charging that undue political meddling by the Klein government and bribery were behind a $420 million loan guarantee given to Triple Five Corporation by the ATB's former acting superintendent. Without the guarantee, the Ghermezians faced losing the mall to their eastern creditors. The lawsuit was finally settled out of court in 2002 with none of the bank's allegations ever proved.

West Edmonton Mall today spans 48 city blocks and has cost $1.2 billion dollars to build. It employs 24,000 people and attracts up to 20 million visitors a year. Construction isn't over yet. Once the ATB lawsuit was settled, Triple Five Corporation committed to another $145-million-dollar expansion to be completed over the next ten years.

Triple Five Corporation today is a conglomerate of almost 400 companies with offices around the world. In the mid-1980s, the Ghermezians took the mega-mall to the United States, building the Mall of America in Bloomington, Minnesota. The shopping and entertainment centre has over 525 stores, employs 12,000 people and is the most visited destination for U.S. travellers, drawing more visitors than Disneyworld, Graceland and the Grand Canyon combined.

The Ghermezians are proposing to double the size of the Mall of America, which would make it the largest mall in the world, at a cost of over one billion dollars. The catch is that the owners want permission to build a casino as part of the billion-dollar expansion. That bid is expected to be put to a city-wide plebiscite.

The Ghermezians also have over 34 companies registered in Nevada. Triple Five affiliates are proposing to build the Great Mall of Las Vegas, starting with more than 2 million square feet of stores and entertainment space at a cost of $300 million.

Eksander (front) and Raphael (behind) Ghermezian

The sons of the brothers Ghermezian now are taking ever more senior roles in Triple Five Corporation and its affiliates. A new generation is preparing to steer this massive development company into the future. For better or worse, the Ghermezians have changed the urban landscape of North America.

John Patrick Gillese

John Patrick Gillese was a prolific Alberta writer who in his later years headed the Literary Arts Branch of Alberta Culture. In his 13-year stewardship, Gillese played an important role in stimulating the emergence of a vibrant made-in-Alberta writing community.

Gillese was born in Omagh, County Tyrone, on March 23, 1920. At age six he came with his family to homestead near Rochefort Bridge, Alberta. As devout Roman Catholics, his parents fled with their three sons to escape the sectarian violence of Northern Ireland. The Catholic faith and the terrible poverty he experienced in Ireland and on the homestead influenced him deeply throughout his life.

As a teen, he ran a successful trapline, using the money raised by selling pelts to supplement the meager family income. The meat of the animals became the main source of the family's diet. Working the trapline throughout the long Alberta winters instilled in him an abiding respect for nature and its creatures. The experience later informed much of his writing.

For years, the thin and gangly Gillese evaded his farm chores and poured his energy into creative writing. He shared his passion for writing only with his mother, for his father thought all such endeavours nonsense. In 1939, at the age of 19, he sent a short story to an American magazine and won $1000 for the contribution. Thereafter, his father allowed him the privilege to write.

He earned his living as a freelance writer through the 1940s and 1950s, penning over 5000 articles, short stories and columns in periodicals in Canada, the U.S. and the United Kingdom. His first book of short stories came in 1957, *Kirby's Gander*. The title short story was made into a 1961 movie called *Wings of Chance*, the first full-length feature film ever made in Canada. Gillese himself played a cameo role as a bush pilot searching the Canadian wilderness for a downed Red Kirby.

Gillese also worked as a literary editor, collaborating with W.G. Hardy on *The Alberta Golden Jubilee Anthology* of 1955 and editing *Chinook Arch*, a Canadian centennial collection of works by Alberta writers, in 1967.

Gillese's own writings earned him the Canadian Author Association's Vicky Metcalf Award in 1967, for contribution to children's literature, and the Allan Sangster Award in 1971, for service to the Canadian Authors' Association. In 1995, the Writer's Guild of Alberta gave Gillese a lifetime achievement award.

Gillese greatly contributed to western Canadian literature through his leadership of the Literary Arts Branch. Alberta became the first province in Canada to have a culture department when the Conservatives under Peter Lougheed took power in 1971. Gillese's role was to stimulate and support Alberta's writing community. He took a populist approach to his portfolio, not viewing literary writing as solely the purview of the university educated. Through contests and workshops, everyday Albertans were encouraged to take up the pen and become writers.

Gillese and the branch can take credit for nurturing the careers of such writers as Fred Stenson, Pauline Gedge and L.R. Wright. In 1975, Gedge, for example, won the Search-for-a-New-Alberta-Novelist competition, co-sponsored by the Literary Arts Branch of Alberta and Macmillan Canada. The victory resulted in the publication of the novel and the launch of her phenomenally successful career. In interviews, she still affectionately mentions Gillese as giving her the confidence that she needed to become the internationally recognized writer she has become. The branch also supplied scholarships so that new writers could attend the Banff Centre for the Arts and study with such literary luminaries as W.O. Mitchell and Alice Munro.

Gillese retired from the Literary Arts Branch in 1986. Soon after, he published *Western Gold: A Heartwarming Collection of Short Stories from the Canadian Northwest*, a book of his own short stories about the homesteaders who opened northern Alberta in the 1920s and 30s. A couple of the stories in *Western Gold* are autobiographical. "The Kiplings" and "The Enchanted Summer" tell of Gillese's childhood in the northern forests. In 1997 this book was reprinted under the title *Fireside Stories*.

After retirement, Gillese continued to write extensively, writing regular columns and editing for various Catholic magazines. calling his craft "a disease I can't leave alone." He also taught creative writing. After a series of strokes, his saddest moment came when he realized that he could no longer write. John Patrick Gillese died in his sleep at the age of 79 on October 23, 1999, in Edmonton.

Lois Hole

On a cold day in mid-January 2005, 2000 Albertans bundled into Edmonton's Francis Winspear Centre for Music to bid a fond and reluctant farewell to a beloved friend and the province's 15th lieutenant-governor, Lois Hole. Thousands more watched the public memorial service on television. The service wasn't simply the formal acknowledgment of the passing of a community leader. It was an outpouring of genuine love and appreciation for a remarkable Albertan.

Twelve days earlier, the 71-year-old lieutenant-governor had finally succumbed to a two-year fight against stomach cancer. Shortly before her death, Lois, as she was simply called by most who greeted her, was asked how she'd like to be remembered. She answered, "I hope that Albertans associate my name with fond memories and good thoughts." No one doubted but that her wishes would be answered.

Lois had the rare quality of touching humans on both an intimate and grand scale with her warmth, kindness and generosity. Dubbed the "Queen of Hugs" by the media, she would indeed hug anyone and everyone within arms' reach. Lois declined to stand on protocol, whether she was the Queen's representative in Alberta, the Chancellor of the University of Alberta, or simply the country girl who watched over the Hole family gardening empire.

Lois Hole was born in 1933 in Buchanan, Saskatchewan. Her family moved to Edmonton when Lois was 15 and she finished her secondary education at Strathcona Composite High School. Lois met her future husband Ted at a Faculty of Agriculture dance when she was 17. She put aside her own ambitions for a university education, as well as a childhood vow that she'd never marry a farmer, and married Ted Hole in 1952. That same year the couple bought a mixed farm in St. Albert. By 1960, the young family was running a vegetable and mixed garden business, which was incorporated as Hole's Greenhouses and Gardens Limited in 1979. Today Hole's Greenhouses, now run by Ted and Lois' sons Bill and Jim, is one of the largest retail greenhouse operations in western Canada.

Raising a family and building the business were demanding enough, but that didn't keep Lois from being equally active in community service. She served for over three decades as a trustee on St. Albert-area school boards and was a member of the Athabasca University Governing Council. She was a fervent believer in the value of education and in the need for strong public support of the education system.

In 1993, Lois took what she'd learned on the farm and wrote the first of 19 best-selling gardening books that established her as a leading gardening authority across Canada and much of the northern United States. The celebrity from her books resulted in her travelling and speaking to audiences across the continent.

In 1998, Lois was appointed Chancellor of the University of Alberta. A year later she was named to the Order of Canada.

Lois Hole became lieutenant-governor of Alberta in February 2000, the second woman to hold that office. While the role is seen as largely ceremonial, Lois continued to speak out on issues she cared most about, such as education, the arts, public health care and caring for the less fortunate. Of her role, Hole said, "While the position of lieutenant-governor is not a platform for activism, neither is it one without substance. My primary goal is to encourage people to carefully consider our more vital issues of social justice, in the hopes that positive change may result."

Among Lois Hole's final projects was the launching of the Lois Hole Library Legacy Program. The program, set up in 2003, encourages the public to donate books to their local libraries in lieu of gifts to others. In its first year of operation, the program raised $117,000 for library acquisitions. In November 2004, a wing at the Royal Alexandra Hospital in Edmonton was named the Lois Hole Hospital for Women.

Following Lois' death, her family established the Lois Hole Care and Nurture Legacy Fund, which disburses money to assist arts organizations, public libraries, the disadvantaged and any group that serves the public good. Within weeks, public donations to the fund had topped $200,000.

Lois herself always spoke with optimism for the future, and her words are worth remembering. "I have faith in a better future, because I have faith that most human beings want to do the right thing. If we can put aside differences of ideology, if we can learn to love one another, then one day we will enjoy a world where no one need live in fear, where no one need go hungry, where everyone can enjoy a good education, the fellowship of friendly neighbours, and the security of a world at peace with itself at long last."

Alex Janvier

Painter Alex Janvier doesn't like it when other aboriginal people call him an "apple"—red on the outside but white on the inside. "It's not an easy title to live with," he says.

But he also recognizes the truth behind the insult. Janvier spent his formative years at the Blue Quills Indian Residential School. There, he was systematically stripped of his aboriginal identity and assimilated into white culture.

Ironically, the residential school system also gave Janvier a profound gift. A priest at the school, Father Rolande, recognized and nurtured the young student's talent for art.

As an adult, Janvier emerged as one of Canada's most acclaimed artists. Along the way, he also became a powerful and eloquent voice for the aboriginal experience in Canada.

Alex Janvier was born in 1935 at the Cold Lake First Nation, near the town of Cold Lake, Alberta. At the time, the Dene Suline people still pursued a traditional First Nations economy of hunting and trapping. Then, in 1954, the Canadian government expropriated their land for the Primrose Air Weapons Range, relocated them to a reserve and effectively destroyed their way of life.

Despite the plight of his people and the trials of his upbringing, Janvier retained a strong sense of his roots. He also continued to paint. In 1960 he earned a degree from the Alberta College of Art, and in 1967 he gained renown for his mural in the Indians of Canada Pavilion at Expo '67 in Montreal.

In 1971, Janvier decided to paint full-time. Two years later, he and six other artists founded Professional Native Artists, Inc. (thus earning the good-natured nickname "Canada's Indian Group of Seven").

Over the years, Janvier's work became both more personal and more political. In the late 1980s, he created his "Apple" series of paintings, confronting his own fractured sense of cultural identity.

In 1995, Janvier painted what many consider his masterpiece: *Morning Star*, a huge mural (19 metres in diameter) on the domed ceiling of the Grand Hall at the Canadian Museum of Civilization.

At the time, however, Janvier remained worried and frustrated over the ongoing struggle of Cold Lake's Dene Suline people. In 1993, the Indian Claims Commission decided overwhelmingly that the First Nation treaty rights had been violated in the 1954 expropriation. Since then, settlement negotiations had been proceeding at a glacial pace.

Finally, in March 2002, the federal government and the Cold Lake First Nation finally reached a land claim settlement. The Dene Suline were awarded $25.5 million in compensation, and their reserve was expanded by 5000 acres.

Later that year, Janvier received the greatest personal honour of his career: a 2002 National Aboriginal Achievement Award.

As Alberta approaches its centenary, Janvier continues to live in Cold Lake and to paint. A bout of Bell's palsy permanently limited his mobility, but he has (characteristically) incorporated the difficulty into his work. Physically unable to execute the strong, bold lines of his earlier work, he now paints softer, airier pictures in watercolour. In 2003, he opened the Janvier Art Gallery in a former Cold Lake bank building.

Yutetsu Kawamura

Life wasn't easy for anyone during the Great Depression in western Canada, but Japanese Canadians had it harder than most, suffering prejudice and cultural isolation as well as poverty. Their troubles, unfortunately, didn't end with the Depression. During World War II, many Japanese Canadians were treated as enemy aliens—stripped of their property and banished to internment camps. Yet, somehow, they endured, with dignity, resilience and profound courage. Consider the example of Reverend Yutetsu Kawamura.

Kawamura was born in Japan in 1908. His father was a Buddhist minister and young Yutetsu, like many Japanese sons, followed in his father's footsteps. When he graduated in 1931, he was given an almost inconceivable assignment: minister to the small, scattered Buddhist communities of the Canadian prairies. In 1934, he and his wife Yoneko set sail for a distant, unknown shore.

After a train ride from Canada's West Coast, the Kawamuras were pleasantly surprised by the Lethbridge train station. This new home, it seemed, was going to be relatively modern and comfortable. Their relief was short lived, however. Their posting was actually in the tiny village of Raymond, 34 kilometres away, down a primitive, muddy road.

It was the height of the Depression. Kawamura, in his diary, wrote, "Dry. I never knew how awful the word 'dry' could be. Most farmers harvested less than they sowed. Many of them couldn't afford to feed pigs any more. When the price of pigs plummeted, they had no choice but to kill them. We didn't even have money to buy coal for cooking or heating, so the youth members of the temple went to an exposed coal seam on the Indian Reserve and dug up the coal that we used all winter long."

Later, during the war, many
displaced Japanese Canadians
came west to Alberta to try
their luck. The local Japanese
Canadians did their best to
absorb and support them, even
though they faced hardships of
their own. Kawamura found
himself becoming a community
leader. He worked hard to preserve Japanese culture, opening
Japanese language schools and
even a co-op Japanese grocery.

After the war, nearly 4000
Japanese Canadians were "repa-
triated" (some prefer the term
"deported") to Japan, even
though many were Canadian
citizens. Reverend Kawamura
was permitted to stay, but only after Senator William A. Buchanan
intervened on his behalf.

The road to full acceptance proved long and slow. In 1948,
Japanese Canadians were finally given the right to vote. Nearly two
decades later, in 1967, race was officially eliminated as a factor in the
immigration process.

That same year, Kawamura found himself front and centre at the
official opening of Lethbridge's centennial project. For many years,
Kawamura had dreamed of building a Japanese garden in his
adopted province. It turned out that Cleo Mowers, publisher of the
Lethbridge Herald, had the same idea. Mowers saw it as a way to honour the Japanese Canadians who had remained in Alberta despite
their hardships. The city's tourism manager, Kurt Steiner, became
involved, and Kawamura's dream blossomed. The Nikka Yuko
Japanese Garden has now been open to the public for nearly four
decades, and ranks among Lethbridge's top attractions.

Kawamura's immense contributions have been recognized in both his country of birth and his adopted homeland. In 1985 he was adopted into the Order of Canada. He received a Japanese Emperor's medal in 1986, and an honorary doctorate from the University of Lethbridge in 1987.

Like his garden, Reverend Kawamura truly took root and flourished here in Alberta.

Ralph Klein

If Ralph Klein's political career began with Ralph cast as the "Rocky" of Canadian politics, today he's the Godfather, and preparing to make his exit from the political stage after serving for more than a decade as the premier of the wealthiest province in Confederation.

Ralph Philip Klein was born in Calgary on November 1, 1942, the son of a wrestler and road contractor. His parents separated when Ralph was six years old, and Ralph was raised by his mother and maternal grandparents in north Calgary.

Klein quit high school at 17 and joined the air force. He served a year and a half before returning to school. He subsequently ran a business college, spent a few years in public relations and then became a television reporter. His 11 years in front of the camera for CFCN Television gave Klein a front row seat in observing the political process. It also gave him a public profile, something he turned to good advantage when he ran for the mayor's job in Calgary in 1980. To the surprise of many, Klein won the election. He went on to enjoy landslide re-elections in 1983 and 1986.

Klein demonstrated a capacity for on-the-job learning early in his career. As he had used his experience as a reporter to master the political process, Klein used his time at Calgary city hall learning how to govern. After nine years in the mayor's chair, Klein ran as a Conservative under Don Getty in the 1989 provincial election. He won his seat and within a month was named Environment minister.

Klein didn't have to wait long to further develop his political ambitions. Wrestling with a deep economic recession and faced with increasing criticism over his leadership, Premier Getty retired from politics in 1992. In the battle for power that followed, Klein portrayed himself as a no-nonsense populist who could turn the party's ailing fortunes around. Backed by the party's right wing, Klein maneuvered a second ballot victory over Nancy Betkowski to take the party's top job. On December 14, Klein was sworn in as premier of Alberta.

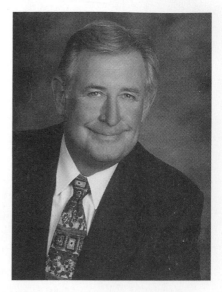

Klein didn't have much time to bask in the warm glow of victory. An election was not far away and many were still betting the Conservatives would lose, in part because new Liberal leader Laurence Decore was effectively pounding the government over its spending record. Klein immediately took a number of high-profile steps aimed at curbing what he termed the province's runaway debt, effectively stealing the fiscal conservative platform from Decore. The new premier and his party managed to get elected the following June.

No one realized it at the time, perhaps not even Klein himself, but he was about to launch a revolution in government. Declaring war on public debt and repeating the mantra that government has no business being in business, the Klein administration began an aggressive program of cost-cutting in health care, education and welfare. It began privatizing many services and assets that historically were held by the government, such as electricity generation, liquor stores and vehicle registrations. At the same time, it deregulated natural gas and electricity prices.

Critics howled that Klein was going too far and simply creating chaos. Thanks in good measure to program cuts and rising oil and gas revenues, the government did indeed move closer to a balanced budget; however, skyrocketing electricity prices, hospital bed shortages, ballooning class sizes and desperate poverty for some were the side effects. Despite growing protests, Klein defused public anger largely through his personable, folksy style. Not that he didn't sometimes show a recklessness that was baffling.

During the first week of the 2004 Alberta election campaign, Klein clashed with a couple of recipients of a government aid program for the severely handicapped, publicly humiliating them and suggesting he'd be quick to cut off aid to anyone who was faking their disability. The remarks resulted in an immediate backlash from disability organizations.

During a debate over whether auto insurance in Alberta should be government run, Klein suggested the socialist policies of Chilean president Salvador Allende had forced Augusto Pinochet to mount a coup. Chilean immigrants in Alberta were furious and several hundred demonstrated on the steps of the legislature to vent their rage.

The incident that most dogged Klein occurred just before Christmas 2001, when an apparently inebriated premier walked into a shelter for homeless men in Edmonton, yelled at the residents to "get a job" and threw money at them. Soon after this incident, Klein appeared in front of news reporters to admit that he had a long-standing drinking problem.

On Monday, November 22, 2004, Ralph Klein led his provincial Conservatives to a fourth majority government. The premier has said this is his last term in office.

Myrna Kostash

Myrna Kostash is a prominent writer, feminist and activist of Ukrainian Canadian heritage who was born, and continues to make her home, in Edmonton. Her journey has been the journey of many contemporary Canadians, although more eloquently expressed than most: the search for one's identity among the influences of ethnic origin, changing gender-based roles and the peer consciousness of a modern, urban generation.

Kostash has evolved a unique nonfiction writing style that she says alternates between point-of-view journalism and creative nonfiction. Her work has been critically praised for its extensive historical and literary research.

Her political activism emerged when she was a student studying Slavic languages and literature at the University of Alberta in the 1960s. Kostash went on to earn her Master's degree in Russian literature from the University of Toronto in 1968. She then went to Europe for a couple of years, where she decided that she wanted to be a writer. While overseas, Kostash began writing for such Canadian magazines as *Saturday Night* and *Maclean's*. Upon her return to Toronto in 1971, she continued her freelance writing career. An assignment for *Miss Chatelaine* magazine led her to become one of the first lecturers at the University of Toronto's Women's Studies program.

Kostash returned to Alberta and her Ukrainian Canadian roots in 1975 to begin research on what would become *All of Baba's Children*. The book, which was published in 1978 by Hurtig Publishers, achieved national acclaim. It expressed the estrangement she felt from her cultural heritage, and explored the pressures and conflicts that have faced Ukrainian Canadians during their history in the New World. Years later, Kostash confessed that the critical perspective she applied to the Ukrainian Canadian community in that book failed to truly comprehend the historic suffering of the Ukrainian people under Soviet dictator Josef Stalin.

Kostash wrote her second book, *A Long Way From Home*, in 1980. In this book, she explored the second significant cultural influence in her life: the 1960s generation that spawned Flower Power and intense civil rights and student activism. *No Kidding: Inside the World of Teenage Girls* followed in 1987, an exploration of the values of a generation younger than her own.

Kostash spent much of the 1980s and early 1990s travelling to Eastern Europe as the Iron Curtain disintegrated. Her travels and research culminated in the publishing of *Bloodlines* in 1993. In this best-seller, she remedied her earlier literary injustice and paints a searing portrait of Stalin's attempted genocide of the Ukrainian people through an engineered famine.

Kostash followed *Bloodlines* with an unusual and intimate homage to the dissident political outlaw entitled *The Doomed Bridegroom*, published in 1998. In 2000, she completed *The Next Canada: In Search of Our Future Nation*. As she had trekked Europe to write *Bloodlines*, so this time she crossed Canada, interviewing Canadians under the age of 35 regarding their expectations, fears and ideals about the nation in which they were coming of age. Once again, the book finds Kostash exploring how people identify themselves through their ethnicity.

Kostash has often felt at odds with the Ukrainian Canadian community, which has been understandably anti-communist and usually conservative in its politics. Kostash is left-of-centre in her political posture and strongly committed to social justice.

In 1993–94, Kostash was Chair of the Writers' Union of Canada, and she has served as writer-in-residence at a number of institutions in Canada and the United States, including the University of Alberta in 2003–04. Her extensive writings, as well as her public lectures across the country, have contributed significantly to the modern debate on multiculturalism in Canada.

Normie Kwong

The life of Normie Kwong has had its share of firsts: the first Chinese Canadian ever to play in the Canadian Football League, the first Chinese Canadian ever to become lieutenant-governor of Alberta, the only person—period—to wear both Grey Cup and Stanley Cup rings.

Lim Kwong Yew was born in Calgary in 1929, one of six children. His parents had emigrated from Canton, China, in the early 1900s. Chinese immigrants were not made to feel welcome in those days: they faced a $500 head tax to come into the country; federal immigration legislation actively sought to bar them; and they were not allowed to hold certain jobs, couldn't buy land or own property and did not have the right to vote. Lim Kwong Yew's father arrived in

Canada with nothing more than a single bag that carried the silver coins needed to pay the head tax.

Chinese Canadians finally got the right to vote in 1947, one year before a talented 18-year-old athlete by the name of "Normie" Kwong managed to land a position as fullback with the Calgary Stampeders of the Canadian Football League. Kwong had discovered his talent with the pigskin while attending Western Canada High School in Calgary.

1948 was a golden year for the Stamps; that year the team took the train to Toronto, complete with chuckwagons and a few hundred crazed Calgary football fans, and won the Grey Cup. Kwong became the youngest player in CFL history to share in winning the Cup.

Kwong spent three years with Calgary before being traded to the Edmonton Eskimos. In Edmonton, Kwong, along with Don Getty, Rollie Miles, Johnny Bright and Jackie Parker, formed the dream team that won three Grey Cups in a row in 1954, 1955 and 1956. In addition to all those Grey Cup rings, Kwong also picked up the nickname "The China Clipper." Ever the comic, Kwong simply referred to himself as "the living legend."

Kwong retired from the CFL in 1960. By that time he held over 30 CFL records. He'd twice been voted the CFL's most outstanding Canadian player and, in 1955, was voted Canada's Athlete of the Year. He had played in seven Grey Cup finals, winning four of them. Kwong ran for over 9000 yards and scored 77 touchdowns over the course of his 13-year professional football career. He still holds the number four spot in the list of the league's all-time rushing leaders. In 1968, Kwong was inducted into the CFL Hall of

Fame. Honours in the Canadian Sports Hall of Fame followed in 1975 and the Alberta Sports Hall of Fame in 1980. Kwong was inducted into the Order of Canada in 1998.

After football, Normie Kwong returned to Calgary where he and his wife Mary raised four sons. He took up a successful career in commercial real estate, eventually becoming vice-president and general manager of Torode Realty. He also remained active in the community, including serving as National Chairman of the Canadian Consultative Council on Multiculturalism in 1979 and 1980. Kwong has remained a popular dinner speaker across Canada over the years and has frequently trekked across the country to fulfill engagements on behalf of nonprofit organizations.

Kwong returned to football in 1988, when he took over as general manager of the Calgary Stampeders, holding that position for three years. He is credited with turning around the fortunes of the Stampeders when they were close to bankruptcy. Kwong also was a co-owner of the NHL's Calgary Flames from 1980 to 1994. When the team won the Stanley Cup in 1989, Kwong became the first person to have won both a Grey Cup and a Stanley Cup.

In the spring of 2005, the immensely popular lieutenant-governor of Alberta, Lois Hole, passed away. Public speculation immediately turned to who could possibly fill her shoes. The federal government announced that it was appointing Normie Kwong as the Queen's Representative in the province. Prime Minister Paul Martin said of Kwong that he "is an inspiration for many Canadians. His many contributions, as a professional athlete, as a business person and as a prominent figure in society, speak to his commitment to the people of Alberta."

As Kwong prepared to take high office, it wasn't clear if he'd be living in Edmonton or in Calgary. After all, the government had just torn down the aging official residence of the lieutenant-governor in the capital city. Asked what he thought might happen, Kwong's humour once again came to the fore. "I don't know what they plan to do—maybe set me up a tent on Jasper Avenue or something."

k.d. lang

Songstress extraordinaire Kathryn Dawn Lang—or k.d. lang, as she is known to the world—was born in Edmonton in November 1961, the youngest of four children. Her family moved to Consort in east-central Alberta when lang was six months old. As a child, she took an interest in piano, guitar and sports.

lang discovered her musical voice early, writing her first song when she was 13. She sang at weddings and at her high school graduation. She attended Red Deer College, majoring in music and theatre. At the time, lang was deeply absorbed in the music of Patsy Cline and jumped at the opportunity to perform in a musical about Cline at the college. After finishing school, she headed to Edmonton, where she immersed herself in performance art and feminism.

One day lang answered a newspaper advertisement for a band seeking a country singer. The ad had been placed by promoter and entertainment manager Larry Wanagas, who recognized immediately that lang was an extraordinary vocal talent, and he worked with her to strengthen her act. lang put together a band called the *re-clines* as a tribute to Patsy Cline and even began to tell audiences that she was the reincarnation of the late American singer.

lang's stage persona in the early 1980s was distinctive and consistent with her experience as a performance artist: a fancy cowboy shirt with abundant fringe, either a denim dress or something wildly splayed and frilly, and cowboy boots to complete the outfit. She would whirl around the stage like a mad dervish (lang says she learned to dance by watching crows). All the while her amazing voice would belt out her self-styled "torch and twang" compositions. Audiences were enthralled.

In 1984, lang recorded her first album for Bumstead Records (Wanagas' label) entitled *A Truly Western Experience*. Two singles from the album and matching videos began to get attention from Canadian campus radio stations and MuchMusic. The album won for lang a 1985 Juno Award for Most Promising Female Artist. The eccentric entertainer showed up to accept the award in a wedding dress.

Soon U.S. record companies were paying attention, with Sire Records signing her in 1986. Her first album with Sire, *Angel With A Lariat*, was critically acclaimed and became both a hit in Canada and an underground hit in the U.S. The album was a mix of 1950s-styled ballads, kitschy rockabilly and honky tonk.

lang faired better with mainstream country fans on her next album, *Shadowland*, recorded in Nashville in 1987 by Pasty Cline's producer, Owen Bradley. Meanwhile, a single released that year featured a duet by lang and Roy Orbison, singing his famous song "Crying." The track was a hit, and lang began receiving serious attention stateside. She cemented her success the very next year with the Grammy-award winning album *Absolute Torch and Twang*.

Even as lang achieved music stardom, she was quick to demonstrate that her individuality and personal beliefs were not up for sale. In 1990, lang was poster girl for an anti-meat campaign launched by the group People for the Ethical Treatment of Animals. The pitch didn't go over well back in Alberta, and in particular her hometown of Consort.

lang followed this media sensation with the revelation that she is a lesbian. The announcement came as lang was about to release her fourth album. lang had yet another surprise in store, however, as *Ingenue* wasn't a country album at all, but a collection of adult contemporary pop songs. The album's first single, "Constant Craving," hit the U.S. Top 40 music charts and provided lang with another Grammy Award. This shift demonstrated lang's fearless determination to follow her muse wherever it lead and trust that her fans would follow.

The release of *Invincible Summer* in 2000 showed lang creating a theme album that sought to capture the feel of endless summer. "It was like rediscovering the happy, optimistic side of myself that I lost touch with in the stress and confusion of maintaining a career," lang said of the album. lang toured with crooning legend and close friend Tony Bennett in 2001 and then, in 2003, paired with Bennett to release the Louis Armstrong tribute album *A Wonderful World*.

By 2004, lang was off in another direction, releasing an homage to Canadian singer/songwriters entitled *Hymns of the 49th Parallel*.

k.d. lang today remains very much in demand as a performer around the world. The woman who has spent most of her life in the spotlight says that growing up in a small town in Alberta prepared her for fame, "Everyone's known my business all my life, so it was no big revelation or sacrifice."

Nickelback

Every small-town kid who ever owned an electric guitar has had the same dream: to find that one song, that one morsel of irresistible Rock God genius, that will propel him from the depths of his parents' basement to the top of the worldwide charts. At the turn of the 21st century, a bunch of guys from Hanna, Alberta, got to live that dream.

The band was Nickelback, and the song was "How You Remind Me," from their 2001 album *Silver Side Up*. For only the second time in history, a Canadian band owned the number one single in both the U.S. and Canada (the only other band to do it was the Guess Who, with "American Woman" in May 1970). In fact, in 2001, "How You Remind Me" was played more often on American radio than any other song. During one particular week, according to industry statistics, "How You Remind Me" was heard more often than any other rock song in history.

Like most "overnight" successes, Nickelback's vault to superstardom was years in the making. They started out as a small-time cover band in 1995, calling themselves the Village Idiots. Chad Kroeger sang lead and played guitar, with his brother Mike on bass, his cousin Brandon on drums, and their pal Ryan Peake on guitar.

A year later, Chad borrowed $4000 from his stepfather, and the boys headed down the road to Vancouver to record a few original

songs. While there, Mike picked up a job at Starbucks and, according to legend, came up with the band's new name. Customers would buy a latté for $1.45, give Mike $1.50, and he'd give them "a nickel back."

The band's first EP, *Hesher*, sold well enough that they decided to record a complete album. *Curb* brought them greater success, selling about 10,000 copies and generating some local airplay and even a bit of exposure on MuchMusic.

They followed that up with a third CD, *The State*, in January 2000. By then, Brandon Kroeger had left the band. After a brief stint with another drummer, the band replaced him with Ryan Vikedal.

As luck would have it, *The State* came out at the same time that Canadian content requirements were increased, sending radio stations across the country scrambling for new product. That, combined with the band's relentless performance schedule, powered the album up the charts. With "Leader of Men" Nickelback had its first bona fide hit. The album also won the group its first U.S. record deal, with Roadrunner Records. *The State* eventually went gold in the US, with sales topping 500,000.

That kind of success attracts serious investment. For their next album, Nickelback was able to hire producer Rick Parashar and mixer Randy Staub, two of the biggest names in metal. The result was *Silver Side Up*, an album that generated three number one singles and sales in the jaw-dropping neighbourhood of ten million so far. In 2003, Nickelback followed up with *The Long Road*, another multiple-platinum hit.

Of course, success can also bring turmoil. Early in 2005, as Nickelback was preparing to record its next album, Ryan Vikedal announced that his bandmates had abruptly fired him. The precise reasons behind the split remain murky. Vikedal was replaced by Daniel Adair, the former drummer for Three Doors Down, a band that Nickelback had toured with in 2004.

As Nickelback enters its second decade, it remains to be seen whether the boys from Hanna can maintain their remarkable momentum. Whatever happens, they have already left an indelible mark on Canadian rock music.

Jean Paré

Simple food, quickly and easily prepared, can be among life's fundamental pleasures. It can also provide the foundation of a publishing empire, as Jean Paré has proven. Although she was 54 years old when she released her first *Company's Coming* title, Paré has gone on to sell millions of books.

During the Depression, in the tiny Alberta town of Irma, home cooking formed the centre of both family life and social life, remembers Paré. "People would come to visit or we would go out to visit, and it was always for a meal."

Her parents often encouraged her to contribute to the cooking, and even prepare entire meals. By the time she left home, Paré had accumulated a huge collection of family recipes, and had developed a life-long habit of reading cookbooks.

At age 18, she married Clarence Lovig, a travelling salesman. They soon moved to Vermilion to operate an auctioneering business, and to raise their four young children. Although the business flourished, the marriage did not. Lovig was an alcoholic and a problem gambler.

In 1963, Jean volunteered to help a friend who was organizing the 50th anniversary of Lakeland College, formerly the Vermilion School of Agriculture. She ended up catering a dinner for over 1000 guests, coordinating the entire operation from her own kitchen. After that success, she found herself catering other local events. Over time, she decided to devote herself full-time to catering.

In 1966, her husband abandoned the family, leaving Jean with a large mortgage and four children to feed. The business grew steadily, with Jean never satisfied unless most of the plates came back empty. Her talent for cooking also brought her love, as she met and married a loyal customer, Larry Paré.

Year after year, people kept asking her, "Why don't you write a cookbook?" Finally, in 1980, she and her son Grant Lovig formed Company's Coming Publishing.

Confronted by thousands of recipes collected over the years, they decided to begin by focusing on a narrow, specific theme. In 1981, they released their first book, *150 Delicious Squares*. A publishing neophyte, Paré ordered 15,000 copies, not realizing that a normal first printing was one-third that size. When the huge shipment arrived, she drove from bookstore to bookstore, starting in Vermilion and working her way out. Three months later, she was sold out and had to order a second printing.

In 1992, *150 Delicious Squares* became the first *Company's Coming* title to pass the one-million mark in sales. As of 2004, *Company's*

Coming had over 100 titles, and had sold over 22 million cookbooks worldwide. That year, Paré was inducted as a Member of the Order of Canada.

From the beginning, Paré stuck to what she considers the golden rule of cookbooks: never share a recipe you wouldn't use yourself. If a dish is overly fiddly to prepare, or uses exotic ingredients, you won't find it in a Company's Coming cookbook. Instead of sending you off on a futile search for wild chanterelle mushrooms,

Paré is more likely to send you into your own pantry looking for a can of tuna. Although this approach has sometimes earned the disdain of "serious" foodies, it has also won her legions of devoted fans.

Holger Peterson

"Mogul" might seem a strange tag for the president of an Edmonton-based record label. Likewise, "industry giant" might sound like a bit of an exaggeration for a man whose company measures its CD sales in the thousands rather than the millions. But apply these terms to Holger Petersen, and nobody on the Canadian music scene is likely to argue with you.

Holger Petersen was born in Germany but came to Alberta as a boy in the late 1950s. Growing up in Edmonton's Bonnie Doon neighbourhood, Petersen was a rabid music fan right from the beginning. He'd often hop on a bus downtown to buy used 45s from jukebox owners, who would sell five or six for a dollar. He loved to read the names on the labels and dream that, one day, his name would be among them.

After high school, he studied radio and television arts at NAIT. He eventually found his way behind a microphone as a CKUA radio host. His program, *Natch'l Blues,* has been a weekly fixture on CKUA for over three decades. National listeners have also come to know and love him as the host of CBC radio's *Saturday Night Blues.*

Petersen's CKUA gig gave him the opportunity to meet and interview most of the blues artists who came through Edmonton in the '60s and '70s. Among these was legendary harmonica player Walter Horton, who was in town with Willie Dixon's Chicago Blues All Stars. Petersen managed to arrange a meeting with Horton, and the two became friends over half a bottle of scotch whiskey. Before long, Horton was in an Edmonton studio recording an album with local blues band Hot Cottage (Petersen was a former drummer with the group). Petersen shopped the record around, finally landing a distribution deal with London Records.

Petersen quickly developed a taste for music production and distribution. He decided to launch his own label, and in 1976 Stony Plain Records was born. Stony Plain scraped along for the first few years (its corporate headquarters was Petersen's kitchen table). The label began to gain momentum, however, after Petersen's friend and business partner, Alvin Jahns, officially became the business manager.

They nursed the company along into the 1980s, but Petersen still had to look elsewhere for his livelihood. He continued on radio and in 1986 became artistic director of the Edmonton Folk Music Festival (he remained at the festival's helm until 1988).

Then, in 1987, came the turning point. Ian Tyson had recorded an album on his own, called *Cowboyography*, and was planning to distribute it through western-wear stores. Petersen convinced him to let Stony Plain release the album instead. Tyson's simple, heartfelt tunes captured the hearts of the nation, and *Cowboyography* went platinum—over 100,000 copies sold in Canada (it continues to rank among Stony Plain's top sellers). The album rejuvenated Tyson's flagging career and transformed Stony Plain into a success story.

Throughout it all, Petersen has maintained a simple formula: sign artists he respects, and give them room to make their own music. In the words of legendary producer Jerry Wexler (Aretha Franklin, Bob Dylan, Ray Charles and many others), "Holger Petersen has cultivated a stony plain and brought forth wondrous fruit."

John and Barbara Poole

John and Barbara Poole would be the last people to seek recognition for their extraordinary generosity. You won't see them smiling for the cameras, handing an over-sized cheque to a grateful charity. In fact, their recent $5 million contribution toward the construction of the new Edmonton Art Gallery was initially anonymous. They only went public after months of persuasion by the media.

To them, their wealth is as much a product of the community as it is of their own hard work. "People make a lot of money here and then take it out of the country, or even to the coast," John Poole has said. "I believe you should try to help your community if you're for-tunate enough to have that opportunity. I think you should leave something behind."

Neither John nor Barbara came from particularly affluent back-grounds. John Poole was born in Regina, Saskatchewan, in 1916 and Barbara McLeod was born in Coronation, Alberta, in 1929. Their families both relocated during the 1930s in an effort to improve their financial prospects. John's father Ernest thought his company, Poole Construction, might do better in Edmonton. Barbara's father, a small-town doctor, moved his family to Calgary in the hope of building a bigger practice.

Ernest Poole hovered near bankruptcy during the 1930s, but he managed to help pay John's way through university. John graduated in civil engineering in 1937, and worked briefly for the City of Edmonton before joining his father's construction firm. In 1948, he and his brother George bought the company (its prospects had improved considerably since the Depression), and gradually built it into one of Canada's foremost construction companies.

In 1952, Barbara graduated with a degree in interior design from the University of Manitoba. That same year, she met John Poole while on a ski trip to Banff. Within a year, they were married. They raised three children together: Scott, Susan and Peter.

In 1977, John and George sold their company in an innovative deal that turned ownership over to the workers. Today, the company (now called PCL) is collectively owned by 1400 employees.

John and Barbara Poole had always been active in the community, and they became even more so after the sale. Instead of packing up their money and retiring to a tropical island, they stayed in Edmonton and devoted themselves to community service.

A highlight was their work with the Edmonton Community Foundation. In 1989, the foundation was virtually a nonentity. Together with Robert Stollery and John's brother George, the Pooles brought together the funds that got the foundation back onto its feet. Today, the foundation boasts assets of $150 million, and has distributed $45 million to education and charities throughout the city.

The Pooles have a particular fondness for promoting Edmonton's cultural life. Just about every major arts organization in the city has benefited from their generosity at one time or another. But their work extends beyond the arts, and beyond Edmonton's city limits. For example, they are partners in a huge private initiative to protect more than 260 square kilometres of land near Waterton National Park.

The Pooles have been widely honoured for their contributions. John was made an Officer of the Order of Canada in 1996, and in 2004 the couple was jointly inducted into the Alberta Order of Excellence.

Ken Read

Calgary's Ken Read is to Canadian competitive skiing what Wayne Gretzky is to hockey; both one of its top stars and one of its builders. Handsome, bilingual and, in his day, nothing short of a madman on the ski hill, Read was the unofficial leader of the amazing team that came to be known as the Crazy Canucks.

When 17-year-old Ken Read joined the Canadian alpine ski team in 1973, Canadians had little experience and no status on the international downhill circuit. They didn't have much money, either. The down-hillers had to make their way through Europe, event to event, in an old Volkswagen van. The World Cup circuit belonged to the Europeans, and in particular to the Austrians. Even more specifically, it belonged to Franz Klammer who, in 1975, won eight of nine World Cup downhill races.

The race Klammer did not win that year went to the unknown Ken Read who, on December 7, raced with insane determination and speed down the course at Val d'Isere, France, clocking a breathtaking time of two minutes and four seconds. With the win, Read became the first Canadian and the youngest male, at age 20, to win a World Cup downhill championship.

Read and his teammates—Dave Irwin, Dave Murray and Steve Podborski—went on to tear up the World Cup circuit. Their willingness to push themselves to the limit to gain the edge in speed earned them the nickname "Crazy Canucks." At a World Cup race in Schladming, Austria, in December 1978, Read placed first, while his fellow Canadians came in second, seventh and ninth.

Ken Read was named to the Canadian squad for the 1976 and 1980 Olympic Winter Games as well as the 1978 and 1982 Canadian World Championship teams. Read didn't take away medals at the Olympics, but he won five World Cups and earned 14 World Cup medals. He also won seven Canadian national titles.

In March 1983, ten years after Read joined the Canadian alpine ski team, he announced his retirement from competitive skiing. In an interview with CBC's Peter Gzowski, the 27-year old skier said that when one focuses with the intensity necessary to compete at the international level, the fun eventually goes out of it. Read looked back fondly on his time as a Crazy Canuck, but he also took a shot at the lack of funding and support the team had received. "It was fun to take the Europeans on at their own game and beat them with a shoestring budget approach. In actual fact, that was a really hit and miss operation and it was more of a frustration than anything."

Life after skiing continued to be busy for Read. He completed a university degree in economics and built a successful national events management company. Read and his wife Lynda, also an alumnus of the Canadian Alpine Ski Team, were kept equally busy raising their three sons in Calgary.

Read became a member of the Canadian Olympic Association in 1981 and, in 1992, he had the honour of serving as the Chef de Mission for the Canadian team at the Olympic Summer Games in Barcelona, Spain.

On May 23, 2002, Ken Read became president of Alpine Canada, charged with the task of steering Canada's competitive ski program into the future. Upon taking the job with Alpine Canada, the 46-year-old Read declared "Canadians deserve international and Olympic success, and our athletes deserve the financial, coaching, and support resources necessary to become the best in the world."

Read also has been a serious fundraiser for cystic fibrosis research, ever since one of his nephews developed the disease 20 years ago. His annual celebrity ski challenge, conducted at five western Canadian resorts, has raised to date $2.8 million. Ken Read is a member of the Order of Canada and an inductee into the Canadian Sports Hall of Fame.

David Schindler

He has convinced governments in North America and Europe to ban phosphates in detergents. He was the first to prove the effects of acid rain on water systems. His research resulted in municipalities around the world building wastewater treatment facilities. He has been called "the world's greatest living freshwater ecologist."

Dr. David Schindler, Killam Professor at the University of Alberta, is unquestionably one of the world's leading environmental scientists. A pioneer in the study of freshwater lake systems, Schindler was the first scientist to truly grasp how pollution changes lakes. His research has been credited with reversing the deaths of thousands of lakes around the world.

The Midwest farm boy earned his Bachelor of Science degree in zoology from North Dakota State University in 1962. He became a Rhodes scholar at Oxford University, where he earned his doctorate in ecology in 1966.

The 1960s were a time of intense debate in scientific circles as to what was causing the rapid decline of lakes in North America and Europe. Schindler, in his 30s at the time, took a holistic approach to the problem, experimenting with whole-lake studies. He discovered that phosphorous, not carbon as many then suspected, was the key to figuring out why lakes were changing. To conduct his experiments, Schindler founded the now world-famous Experimental Lakes Area near Kenora, Ontario, in 1968. He directed research at the centre, owned by the Canadian Department of Fisheries and Oceans, for over two decades.

In the mid-1970s, Schindler turned his attention to the acidification of freshwater lakes as a result of the pollution carried in rainfall. Schindler proved that even mild acid rain resulted in a significant decline in the biodiversity of lakes. As a direct result of his research, governments around the world introduced bans on sulphur oxide emissions.

In 1989, Schindler became Killam Memorial Professor of Ecology at the University of Alberta in Edmonton, a post he holds to this day. His research in recent years has focused on the lakes of

the boreal forest and specifically the impact of global warming, ozone depletion and acid rain. His work shows that climate warming and drought are having severe and previously unknown effects on the life of lakes. In a 2002 interview with *Outdoor Canada* magazine, Schindler painted a grim portrait of the forests and lakes of western Canada if something isn't done to reverse global warming.

Schindler says as a result of global warming and excessive human consumption of water, flows in the major rivers of western Canada have been reduced to between 20 and 50 percent of their historic flows. He projects freshwater supplies will become increasingly toxic, risking public health and freshwater fish stocks. Schindler charges that a failure to respond to climate warming through such initiatives as the Kyoto accord, and poor freshwater management by all three levels of government, are largely to blame for what will soon be a full-blown crisis.

Schindler has been awarded numerous international scientific honours, and in 2001 was awarded Canada's highest scientific honour, the Gerhard Herzberg Canada Gold Medal for Science and Engineering. "David Schindler is the epitome of the active and engaged scientist," said Gilbert Normand, Secretary of State for Science, Research and Development, in announcing the award. "He is passionate about his research and about conveying to Canadians the importance of science in guiding decisions about the natural world."

Schindler received the Order of Canada in 2004. He is a Fellow of the Royal Society of Canada and the Royal Society of London (UK) and is also a member of the U.S. National Academy of Sciences. Schindler is the author of over 240 research papers, 19 of them published in the world's leading scientific journal, *Nature and Science*.

"Schindler is a role model for many young scientists the world over," says Tom Brzustowski, head of the Natural Sciences and Engineering Research Council of Canada. "He has had an enormous influence beyond his field."

Schindler continues to use that influence to encourage the public and governments to accept the reality of global warming and to find the collective will to do something about it. Those who know him well say Schindler is not alarmist and, while he can appear blunt and brusque, he is simply very honest and fearless.

Horst A. Schmidt

The years of government under Premier Peter Lougheed have been described by author Fil Fraser as "Alberta's Camelot," a period in which the province poured serious money into cultural projects and the arts in general. Roy MacGregor of the *Globe and Mail* wrote of the era, "It was a time when the Banff Centre became a year-round, world-class facility. The Edmonton Symphony became internationally renowned. Calgary got the Glenbow Museum, Edmonton the new Citadel Theatre. The Edmonton Folk Festival, the Heritage Festival and the groundbreaking Fringe Festival all became successes. Alberta even produced the Canadian Encyclopedia, a magnificent production that meant those unappreciative Easterners would at least have something to read in the dark."

If Peter Lougheed and his wife Jeanne were king and queen in this Camelot, then Horst Adolph Schmidt, the government's culture czar, was Merlin.

Horst Schmidt was born in Munich, Germany, in April 1933. He grew up surrounded by music, at least when air raid sirens weren't blowing. At a liberal arts language school, he learned several languages. In high school, he was placed in a machinery design training program, in which the shop foreman taught him to appreciate literature, specifically poetry. After the war, Horst studied at a Jesuit school and joined the Young Christian Workers, a group that fought for workers' rights. He also joined a student opera association.

By the age of 19, Schmidt had decided that Bavaria held no future for him. In 1951, he sold everything he owned and sailed to Quebec City and, from there, travelled by train to Edmonton.

Horst opted to work in a gold mine in Yellowknife, where he could earn what was then a whopping $1.25 an hour. He hadn't learned English at this point but quickly picked it up, although he spoke it with a thick German accent he never really managed to lose. The ever-energetic Schmidt also began to sing and perform in local theatre productions, volunteered at the local radio station and started taking correspondence courses in business from the University of Toronto.

Horst returned to Edmonton in 1956 and went into the import-export business. The enterprise was successful. Horst next partnered with well-known local entertainer Gaby Haas and others to open a restaurant, the Hofbräuhaus. By the early 60s, Horst was travelling around northern and central Alberta selling insurance. Around this time, Horst also hosted a weekly German music program on CKUA Radio, which made him something of a goodwill ambassador for Edmonton's large German community.

In 1965, fellow CKUA announcer Jim Edwards introduced Schmidt to Peter Lougheed, who at the time was campaigning for the leadership of the Alberta Conservative Party. Horst and Lougheed hit it off. Horst ran for the Tories in Edmonton-Avonmore in the 1971 vote and was elected. Ten days later, he was appointed Minister of Culture, Youth and Recreation, becoming the first post-Second World War immigrant to be appointed a Cabinet minister in Canada.

Horst Schmidt took up his new duties with a zeal born of genuine passion, launching new provincially funded initiatives in every art discipline imaginable. In 1972, he convinced the government to mandate the Alberta Foundation for the Arts to spend $50,000 a year buying the art of Albertans, both as a way of encouraging artists and to preserve Alberta culture. Today the collection has 6400 works and is valued at over $9 million. In 1974, he announced that August first was going to become a provincial statutory holiday called Heritage Day. This led directly to creation of the Heritage Day Festival in Edmonton two years later.

Perhaps Schmidt's most important initiative was the Alberta Matching Grants Program, which matched private donations dollar for dollar up to 25 per cent of a cultural organization's budget. This program triggered a significant increase in private sector donations to the arts.

Schmidt's last year as Minister of Culture was 1979. In the preceding eight years, he had increased annual government funding for the arts from $283,000 to more than $7.5 million. He moved from his beloved portfolio to a new assignment as Minister of State for Economic Development and International Trade and could claim credit for bringing many new trade opportunities to the province. His political career finally came to an end when he lost to a New Democrat by 93 votes in the 1986 election.

Horst Schmidt has since returned to the private sector. He remains a familiar sight, however, at cultural and artistic events and celebrations around Alberta—for some, at least, a ghost of Christmas past.

James Shapiro

Dr. James Shapiro was nervous, yet elated. He was about to step to the lectern in front of hundreds of distinguished colleagues, at a meeting of the American Society of Transplant Surgeons and the American Transplantation Society in Chicago. In May 2000, after a year of cautious optimism, Shapiro was ready to unveil the Edmonton Protocol.

Shapiro and his team had taken islet cells, which produce insulin in the pancreas, and injected them into eight patients. The cells migrated to the liver and began to produce insulin. Before the treatment, the patients faced up to 15 insulin injections per day. Now, a year later, they were needle-free.

Shapiro's announcement, and the article that followed in the *New England Journal of Medicine*, marked the greatest single advance in diabetes research since the discovery of insulin.

Shapiro was born in Leeds, U.K., and studied medicine at the University of Newcastle-upon-Tyne and the University of Bristol. As a student, he spent a year studying islet transplantation in rats— although, as he later recalled, "virtually all the experiments were compete failures."

He came to the University of Alberta in 1993, attracted by the school's reputation as a leader in liver transplantation. Once he was there, however, he found himself drawn back into the field of islet transplants.

In 1989, the U of A's Ray Rajotte had become the first Canadian to perform an islet transplant. Since that time, however, islet transplantation had been dismissed as a clinical dead end. Worldwide, 92 percent of subjects returned to injecting insulin within one year.

Shapiro and his team were stumped. "…[W]hy was the transplant procedure in islet transplants such a dismal failure when all other transplant programs enjoyed almost 90 percent success rates?" They decided to come at the problem from a new angle. "It seemed to us that the answer might be in the drugs."

Shapiro focused first on steroids. Steroids help prevent tissue rejection, but they also damage islet cells and raise the body's resistance to insulin. The team developed a new cocktail of three immunosuppressant drugs, and administered them without steroids.

They made other changes as well. They tried their treatment on healthier patients. Until then, islet transplants had only been used with patients who were already suffering kidney failure. Team members Jonathan Lakey and Greg Korbutt worked to improve methods of extracting and refining islet cells from donor pancreases. This allowed the surgeons to use fresh, pure islet cells, rather than cultured or frozen ones.

The combination proved a stunning success. Islet recipients began producing their own insulin immediately, and suffered only minor side effects from the drugs.

At the time of writing, work still lies ahead. Researchers around the world continue to look for better, safer anti-rejection drugs. And in February 2005, Shapiro took part in the first-ever live-donor islet transplant, in which a woman in Japan donated part of her pancreas to her daughter. Until now, every treatment has required two donor pancreases.

With the Edmonton Protocol, James Shapiro and his team awakened new hope in the hearts of millions of diabetes sufferers. Since then, they have continued to work toward delivering on that promise.

The Southerns

A scribe with the *Globe and Mail* recently described the Southern family as "the closest thing Alberta has to landed aristocracy." With a third generation of Southerns now sitting atop the ATCO empire, the family certainly has come to epitomize Alberta's wealthy and powerful. That said, they built it the hard way—from the ground up.

Don Southern began what would become the corporate giant ATCO Group back in 1946. He bought 15 utility trailers in Calgary and started Alberta Trailer Hire Company. Mobile home sales soon followed and the utility trailer business went national. By the 1960s, Don's company was building industrial housing for projects around the world.

Today ATCO Group is a multi-billion dollar, worldwide company involved in involved in electric power generation, transmission and distribution; natural gas transportation, processing and distribution;

Margaret and Ron Southern

technical services and facilities management; energy marketing and services; workforce housing and industrial noise abatement.

Don's son Ron worked with his father right from the start and, as chief executive officer, was largely responsible for ATCO's phenomenal growth. Ron, who reportedly earned over a million dollars a year while at the helm of the company, has now handed the reins of the company over to his daughter Nancy, although he remains chairman of the board.

In 1995, Ron Southern was honoured by Queen Elizabeth, who named him a Commander of the British Empire. He has been a director of the British Canadian Chamber of Trade and Commerce and has worked to improve commercial relations between the two countries. In 1996, he was voted "CEO of the Year" by the *Financial Post*.

Mention the name Southern to most Calgarians and they immediately think of Spruce Meadows, the local show-jumping equestrian facility repeatedly ranked the best in the world by the International Equine Federation. Spruce Meadows was the dream and passion of Ron Southern's wife, Margaret, who had developed a growing interest in equestrian sports.

Margaret Southern grew up in Calgary. She graduated from the University of Alberta in 1953 with a degree in physical education and was the Bakewell Trophy winner that year for top female athlete at the U of A. Returning home, Margaret was the first woman ever hired to teach in what became the University of Calgary's Physical Education department. She also wasted no time becoming a builder in Calgary's recreational sector. Margaret was a founding member of

Calgary's Parks and Recreation Board
and was a leader in developing an aggressive land banking program, so that significant areas of land in Calgary were set
aside for recreational use. She played a
key role in the development of Calgary's
Fish Creek Park, the first provincial park
to be situated inside a city.

The Southerns began building
Spruce Meadows in 1973 and opened
the centre in 1975. The facility was
erected on the site of a former feedlot,

Don Southern

20 kilometres west of downtown Calgary. Today the complex sprawls
across 300 acres of land, featuring almost two dozen buildings, seven
permanent stables, two indoor arenas and a tournament centre. The
best riders and jumping horses in the world come to compete at
Spruce Meadows, in part for the millions of dollars in prize money
up for grabs. The centre attracts 400,000 visitors a year. Broadcasts
from the Spruce Meadows television centre are transmitted to 70
countries with an audience of more than 700 million people.

Right along with the Stampede, Spruce Meadows has put
Calgary on the world map. The facility continues to expand, with a
new grandstand and clock tower being built in 2005, Spruce
Meadows' 30th year of operation.

In recent years, the family has battled to keep developers at bay
who want to take Calgary's suburbs right to the edge of the equestrian centre. Margaret Southern has taken the lead in that fight,
meeting with Calgary's mayor and provincial Cabinet ministers to
try to protect the atmosphere of Spruce Meadows. She rejects any
suggestion that the Southerns might get special treatment because
of their prominence and wealth.

"We're citizens like everyone else, and we just want to try and
make the city better," she told a *Globe and Mail* reporter.

Nancy Southern has been president and chief executive officer of
ATCO Limited since 2003. She was groomed for the role over

many years, from her studies in economics and commerce at the University of Calgary to the first time she became a director of the company in 1989. A mother of three, Nancy Southern competed internationally in equestrian events in the 1970s and 80s. Nancy's sister, Linda Southern-Heathcott, currently serves as executive vice-president of Spruce Meadows, and one day will take over the running of the facility from its current president, her mother Margaret.

If nothing else, the Southerns underscore that while Alberta may be not long from its frontier past, the province has had time enough to build dynasties.

Don Stanley

Donald Russell Stanley could have pursued a career as an athlete if he hadn't been so fascinated with building things—really big things.

Don Stanley started life in Edmonton in October 1917. He went to Eastwood High School and on to the University of Alberta, where he earned a Bachelor of Science in Engineering with distinction.

Stanley was a well-rounded athlete throughout high school and university, playing basketball, football and soccer. He excelled at hockey, and was on the Canadian team in both the 1949 and 1950 World Hockey Championships. Canada won the gold at the 1950 series in England.

During the Second World War, Stanley served in the Royal Canadian Air Force as an engineering officer. After the war, he came back to Edmonton and took a job as director of environmental engineering with the Alberta government. While with the government, he earned his Master of Science degree from Harvard University in 1948 and his doctorate in environmental engineering in 1953.

The next year, Don Stanley opened his own one-man engineering firm, Stanley Associates Engineering. To get started, he mailed 600 letters to potential clients and then drove all over western Canada visiting small communities. He landed a couple of small projects for municipal water and sewer systems and was on his way.

For the next four decades, Don Stanley distinguished himself as a pioneer in environmental engineering, the science and technology of engineering solutions to environmental problems. He was involved extensively in waste management, water supply systems and development of technology to reduce or eliminate pollutants, working on projects around the world. Always an innovator, Stanley was recognized with a number of national engineering  awards. He also was among the founding members of the respected Canadian Academy of Engineering.

In 1983, at age 66, Stanley put Ron Triffo in charge of his firm, at the height of a major slump in the western Canadian economy. The company downsized from 400 to 200 staff to stay in the black. At the same time, Triffo began to refocus the company's business strategy. Triffo initiated an aggressive series of strategic takeovers of other companies, eventually more than 50 firms in all. Triffo, in turn, handed over the reins of the company to Tony Franceschini in 1998, who became just the third CEO of the firm since its founding.

Stantec, as it is now called, now has over 4000 employees in 40 countries around the world. The company has completed over 40,000 projects in 80 countries. Among the many Canadian projects designed by Stantec is the Confederation Bridge that links Prince Edward Island to the mainland, named one of the five most significant Canadian engineering achievements of the 20th century. Stantec also was involved in designing the $209 million Vancouver Skytrain project.

Stanley's remarkable career as an engineer and businessman was matched by his dedication to community service. He sat as president of both the Edmonton and Alberta Chambers of Commerce and was a member of the University of Alberta Board of Governors. He also served on the Alberta Round Table on the Environment and the Economy and was involved with the World Health Organization in matters related to environmental health.

Don Stanley died in September 2001, at the age of 83, after a long battle with Parkinson's Disease. He served as honorary chair of the board of Stantec until his passing.

Robert Steadward

For Robert Steadward, fate was decided in an assignment he was given while a student at the University of Alberta. Little did he know it but that assignment also turned the fate for thousands of disabled athletes around the world.

Bob Steadward was born and raised in Eston, Saskatchewan. He had been athletic in school, and after graduation he headed to the U of A to get his degree in physical education. He was active in varsity track and field and enjoyed coaching. At one point, Steadward was assigned the task of setting up a wheelchair basketball team. He quickly discovered that the challenge was a deeply rewarding experience. He soon was also coaching swimming and track teams for Edmonton's first wheelchair club.

Steadward earned his Bachelor's degree in Physical Education with Distinction and remained at the University of Alberta to complete his Master's degree in Science. A stint at the University of Oregon earned him a doctorate. He returned to Edmonton and was made a professor in the Physical Education department in 1971.

He continued coaching athletes both with and without disabilities. In baseball, he took two teams to national finals, while also coaching high school football and university athletics. Steadward was a national coach for the Canadian Paralympic Committee from 1966 to 1976. He also served as a fitness consultant to both the 1979 Edmonton Oilers and the 1980 Canadian Olympic hockey team.

As a professor, Steadward focused on developing new ways to help disabled athletes achieve their full potential. He specialized in research aimed at adapted physical activity for those who were disabled through amputation or paralysis. In 1978, Steadward founded the Research and Training Centre for Athletes with Disabilities at the U of A, later named the Rick Hansen Centre and, much later, the Steadward Centre.

In 1973, Steadward had met Sir Ludwig Guttman, the man who started paralympic competition immediately after the Second World War as a way of rehabilitating disabled veterans. Steadward was convinced that the rehabilitation model should be replaced with a sports model, where participants trained as athletes first and disabled persons second. He began working toward the creation of an international governing body with a focus on elite sport.

Steadward's goal was achieved in 1989 with the formation of the International Paralympic Committee (IPC). He was named the organization's founding president. Under his stewardship, the IPC's national membership grew from 43 to 160 nations. Steadward held the position until 2001, and remains honorary president of the IPC. He also has sat on the International Olympic Committee and is a member of the Canadian Olympic Committee.

Quite apart from his professional involvement, Steadward has devoted a tremendous amount of volunteer time to coaching and administration, participating at the local, national and international levels. He has helped organize sporting events for athletes with and without disabilities, including Universiade, the Commonwealth Games, the Olympics and the Paralympics. He was co-chair of Edmonton's successful bid for the 2001 World Track and Field Championships. He was a founder of the Alberta Wheelchair Sports Association and the Canadian Sports Fund for the Physically Disabled.

In September 2001, Steadward retired from the University of Alberta, but he didn't stay retired for long. Steadward is director of sports counseling for the Edmonton Sports Institute, a sports medical clinic, and also is business manager and agent for Jamie Salé and David Pelletier, Olympic champions and gold medalists in pairs figure skating. He's a member of the Board of Governors for the 2005 World Masters Games in Edmonton, and he was a member of the Board of Directors for the Vancouver-Whistler Bid Committee to host the 2010 Olympic and Paralympic Winter Games. In recent years, Steadward, a long time fan of rodeo, has been working behind the scenes to try to get the rodeo circuit to function more like other professional sports and to get a better deal for cowboy athletes.

Bob Steadward has been called the father of the modern Paralympics, now the second largest sports organization in the world. For his significant accomplishments, he was made an Officer of the Order of Canada in 1999 and has received numerous other honours from around the world.

Winnifred Stewart

Winnifred Stewart believed passionately that those who were challenged in their mental development had much to contribute to society. The strength of her belief brought lasting, positive changes throughout Alberta and the rest of western Canada.

Winnifred Parker was born in Fernie, British Columbia, in June 1908. Her father worked in the coal mining industry. In 1912, Levi Parker moved his family to Edmonton. Winnifred studied nursing at the Edmonton General Hospital, graduating as a registered nurse in 1929. Three years later, she married businessman Duncan Stewart.

The Stewarts had a son in 1934, but the event was bittersweet. Parker Stewart was born with Down Syndrome, a genetic malfunction that results in mild to severe mental retardation. In Parker's case, the result was severe, and his circumstances were further complicated by diabetes.

All of the doctors and other experts who examined Parker told Winnifred Stewart that his case was hopeless and that she should not expect any improvement. Parker's mother refused to give up and remained determined to do everything in her power to give her son an optimal life. Said Stewart, "First of all I eliminated the words 'can't' and 'impossible' from my vocabulary."

Stewart improvised teaching methods as she went along, taking Parker everywhere with her and involving him in normal life activities. The key was helping Parker to transfer what he learned in one situation to other events in his life. The results were nothing short of miraculous by the standards of the day. Parker could swim by the time he was one and could speak by age six. He also could read at a grade one level and could interact socially.

The next hurdle came when Winnifred Stewart tried to get her son placed in a local school. The principal refused to admit Parker, saying that to attempt to educate him would be futile. Over the next 12 years, Winnifred cared for her son at home and continued to find ways to teach him and help him develop.

By 1953, Winnifred Stewart had met other parents with Down Syndrome children who were just as frustrated as she was by the lack of public support for such children. A small group of them met to figure out how to obtain appropriate education for their children. In March 1953, a group of 60 gathered to form the Organization for the Rehabilitation of Retarded Children, with Winnifred Stewart as the first president. Within weeks, the first class for the mentally handicapped was held in space donated by the city, with 25 students in attendance.

The next year, Winnifred Stewart became the first woman ever to address the Alberta legislature from the floor of the house. As a result of her lobbying, the Alberta government became the first in Canada to provide funding for schools for the mentally handicapped. In 1955, Winnifred Stewart founded the first association in Canada for teachers of the mentally handicapped.

From 1954 through 1970, Stewart founded schools for the mentally handicapped in 19 communities throughout western Canada. Stewart devoted herself to experimental research in learning techniques for the severely mentally handicapped. She became internationally recognized for both the curriculum and teaching methods she pioneered.

Stewart inspired others to take up the cause as well. In 1968, the multi-million dollar Western Industrial Research Training Centre was opened to provide vocational training opportunities. In 1979, Cerwood Industries opened in Edmonton, a vocational training sheltered workshop for the mentally handicapped. Stewart also developed working relationships with 45 school divisions in Alberta that had students attending her schools.

In 1972, Stewart retired as principal of Winnifred Stewart School. That same year she was recognized for her devotion and her accomplishment, named an Officer of the Order of Canada and granted an honorary Doctor of Laws degree from the University of Alberta.

Winnifred Stewart passed away in 1990. Her life insurance policy was paid out to the Winnifred Stewart Association for the Mentally Handicapped in the amount of $400,000, allowing establishment of the Winnifred Stewart Foundation. The foundation today raises funds for the association and for other related organizations.

Winnifred Stewart was a tireless champion for removing the social stigma that had been attached to Down Syndrome children. That such children are more integrated and accepted in the social mainstream today is much to the credit of this stalwart Albertan.

The Sutters

When Louis Sutter passed away in February 2005, newspapers across the country hailed him as "Canada's greatest hockey dad."

There's no disputing that claim. Louie Sutter and his wife Grace raised seven boys on their farm near Viking, Alberta. All of them played hockey, and six of them played in the NHL. It's hard to imagine any family ever coming close to matching the Sutters' astonishing record in the league.

Brian, the second oldest, joined the St. Louis Blues for the 1976–77 season. For the next 25 consecutive years, there was at least one Sutter brother in the NHL—Brian, Duane, Brent, Darryl, Rich and Ron. For a five-year stretch in the 1980s, all six were in the league. Once, in October 1983, four Sutter brothers played in the same NHL game—when the Philadelphia Flyers (Ron and Rich) took on the New York Islanders (Duane and Brent).

The final family tally in the NHL: 4994 regular season games, 603 playoff games, 1320 goals and 1615 assists.

The program at Louie's funeral said that he "was stubborn as a mule and as tough as nails." Apparently, it ran in the family. To a man, the Sutter brothers had a reputation for tenacity, loyalty and physical courage. In the eyes of their fans, they personified the greatest attributes of the Canadian approach to the game.

Left to right, back row: Ronald, Brent, Duane, Richard; front row: Brian, Gary, Darryl

The boys grew up in an 800-square-foot farmhouse with no running water (the family finally moved to a larger farm in 1967). Whenever they had a break from chores, they'd pile into the hayloft for a quick but intense game of shinny. Winter evenings were often spent playing hockey on a frozen slough about a kilometre from the house. They'd play into the night, until their mother Grace honked the horn of the family car to call them in.

Farm life taught the boys the value of both competition and cooperation. They were never allowed to play hockey until their chores and their homework were done. They'd push each other to see who could work the quickest and hardest, and pitch in to help each other when necessary.

There may have been another source of their competitive streak, according to Brian. "We had seven kids and one bathroom. Now that's competition."

When Brian made it into major junior, and then the NHL, he cranked up the sibling rivalry to a new level. From that point on, none of his younger brothers would be satisfied unless they made it as well. They were all skilled players, but were rarely the most talented men on the ice. Instead, they stood out for their sheer determination. They also had a talent for bringing out the best in their teammates; four of them were team captains.

All six of the Sutter brothers who were in the NHL continue to make their living at the game. Two are NHL head coaches: Darryl in Calgary and Brian in Chicago. Brent owns, coaches and manages the Red Deer Rebels (one of Canada's most successful junior clubs), and coached Canada's junior team to the gold medal at the 2005 world championship. Twin brothers Ron and Rich are both NHL scouts.

Another generation of Sutters joined the NHL in 2005 when the Calgary Flames selected Brett Sutter, son of Darryl, as their 179th draft pick. Twenty-seven years earlier, Darryl himself had been the 179th choice.

Eventually, there may no longer be any Sutters in professional hockey. But the Sutter name will continue to inspire Canadian hockey players for generations to come.

Lorne Tyrrell

When he walks down Edmonton's streets, Dr. D. Lorne J. Tyrrell isn't likely to be mobbed by admirers. But the University of Alberta's Dean of Medicine and Dentistry has had a profound and lasting effect on his community and province, and has won acclaim as one of the world's greatest medical minds. His groundbreaking research has helped save thousands of lives.

Tyrrell's roots are planted firmly in Albertan soil. He was born in 1943, and grew up on a farm near Duffield, about 50 kilometres west of Edmonton. After graduating from high school in Stony Plain, he inched a little farther down the road to the University of Alberta. He earned a Gold Medal in Science when he graduated from chemistry in 1964, and four years later earned a Gold Medal in Pediatrics when he graduated from medicine. He moved on to Queen's University for his post-graduate studies, earning a PhD in pharmacology in 1972, before moving back to Alberta to complete his training in internal medicine.

His life's focus changed in 1976, when he received a Medical Research Council of Canada Centennial Fellowship. He used the opportunity to study at Sweden's Karolinska Institute. There, he discovered a lasting passion for the study of viruses.

Tyrrell returned to the U of A to teach and continue his research. In 1986, he and chemistry professor Morris Robins began researching possible antiviral drugs against hepatitis B, which affects over 300 million people worldwide and was, at the time, the ninth leading cause of death. Their work led to the creation of the Glaxo Heritage Research Institute, one of the largest research contracts ever signed by a Canadian university. The drug therapy developed by Tyrrell's team has revolutionized the treatment of hepatitis B.

Tyrrell remains at the forefront of research. In 2001, his team successfully implanted human liver cells into genetically modified mice. Until then, only chimpanzees and humans could be infected with hepatitis C. Now, for the first time, new antiviral drugs against that disease can be tested on small animals.

Tyrrell doesn't spend all of his time in labs, however. Over the years, he has built a reputation as one of Alberta's finest teachers and doctors. Students have voted him "Teacher of the Year" at every level of medical study, and his patients frequently praise his compassionate bedside manner.

In 1994, Tyrrell was made Dean of Medicine at the U of A, and he was reappointed five years later as Dean of Medicine and Dentistry. He has used this higher profile to speak out in support of quality public health care in Canada. He was inducted into Alberta's Order of Excellence in 2000, and named an Officer of the Order of Canada in 2002. In August 2004, the Canadian Medical Association gave him its greatest honour, the F.N.G. Starr Award.

Tyrell's Order of Canada citation nicely sums up his life and career: "He has brought Canada to the forefront of medical research. His work has brought hope to millions of patients as well as international accolades. Equally admired for his teaching abilities and for his great dedication to patients, he is a champion of quality medical health care."

Ian Tyson

Music legend Ian Tyson seems about as tough, durable and craggy-looking as the Rocky Mountains that rise to the west of his Longview ranch. At 71 years of age, the man who has made a life and a career out of doing things his own way and changing direction as best suits him, is showing only a few signs of slowing down.

Tyson was born in Victoria, BC, in September 1933. He was fascinated with cowboy culture and the Old West, likely in part because of the Will James cowboy novels that he loved to read. Tyson's father, who had been a ranch hand in southern Alberta, hoped his son would train as an accountant, but the young man's fancy was drawn to art and rodeo. Tyson's passion for horses resulted in a bad fall in his early 20s. While recuperating in hospital, he began playing a guitar and found he liked it. Tyson went to the Vancouver School of Arts to study graphic arts and began playing music semi-professionally at clubs in and around Vancouver's Chinatown.

After graduating from school in 1958, Tyson headed to Toronto, where he found employment with an advertising company. He also began performing music with a young singer named Sylvia Fricker.

Tyson quickly built a reputation in Toronto as a top-notch illustrator and graphic artist, but that didn't stop him from heading back west for a while to rejoin the rodeo circuit. Back in Toronto after that, Tyson found an exploding folk scene in the district of Yorkville. Tyson and Fricker picked up rehearsing their unique duo sound.

By spring 1961, Ian and Sylvia were among the hottest tickets in Yorkville. That summer they played at the inaugural Mariposa Folk Festival. By autumn, Ian and Sylvia were in New York's Greenwich Village, looking for a record deal. They signed with Vanguard Records. Their debut album opened to rave reviews, and they were soon much in demand on the U.S. college circuit and sold out two concerts at Carnegie Hall. For the couple's second album, Tyson wrote his first song—his most famous—"Four Strong Winds." Ian and Sylvia went on to record over a dozen albums together.

Tyson bought a farm outside Toronto, married Sylvia and had a son. They continued to tour as Ian and Sylvia or as Great Speckled Bird through the 1960s. Tyson also had a television show for four years in the early 1970s broadcast across Canada and in a number of U.S. markets.

But Tyson was becoming disillusioned with the music business. He decided to give it up, at least for the time being, and pursue his first love, handling and training horses. So he moved to a cattle ranch near Pincher Creek, Alberta, and he and Sylvia divorced.

The next two years were largely spent ranching. By 1977, Tyson found himself once again fronting a band and on a performance tour across Canada. His fortunes picked up decidedly when Neil Young covered "Four Strong Winds." The royalty cheques provided the down payment on Tyson's own ranch at Longview in the Alberta foothills.

Tyson split his time between running the ranch and putting some steam back in his music career. He put out an album in 1983 called *Old Corrals and Sagebrush*. It marked the beginning of a string of albums dedicated to the cowboy way of life that Tyson loved. This new phase of Tyson's music career exploded in 1986 with release of the album *Cowboyography*, which achieved platinum status.

He also started a regular gig at the Ranchman's in Calgary, where his attention was caught by a waitress. There was over 20 years difference in age between them and some considered the relationship scandalous. Tyson didn't care, and credited Twylla Dvorkin both with saving his life and kick-starting his second recording career. They tied the knot in August 1986 and went on to have a daughter. Sadly, Tyson recently indicated that he and Twylla are splitting up.

Tyson was named to the Canadian Country Music Hall of Fame in 1989, one of many honours, including being named to the Order of Canada in 1994. Forty years after his first appearance there, Ian Tyson took the stage at the 2001 Mariposa Folk Festival.

Once again, Tyson is touring to get the word out about his new album, *Songs from the Gravel Road*. Given his age and his love for his high country home, one could easily wonder why he still bothers. Tyson says he misses Alberta skies and his ranch when he's on the road but that he "wants to share true stories of a part of Canada too few people know, and the details of lives well lived." The life of Tyson, whose crooning cowboy ways have made him beloved from Alberta to Texas, should certainly be counted among them.

Jon Whyte

Jon Whyte—poet, historian, publisher, columnist, filmmaker and museum curator—has a bright star in the firmament of Alberta's cultural heaven. The *Poetry Canada Review* said of him that he was "one of the two outstanding radical innovators in Canadian poetry."

Jon Whyte also has been called the conscience of the town of Banff. Certainly the mountain community was both his birthplace and the geographic and spiritual centre of his world. Born there in 1941, Whyte spent an idyllic childhood in what was still a small mountain town, without much of the international tourist traffic that marks the community today.

In a piece called "The Secret Banff: The Town Behind the Tourists," Whyte wrote about the Banff he knew as a boy, expressing the mystery of childhood with all the magic and charm of Mark Twain's *The Adventures of Tom Sawyer*. Whyte's memories included the building of tree houses, skinny-dipping in icy lakes, finding porcupines in trees and the smells of the local stables. "You can never hope to visit that Banff, because it can never exist again, though it continues to exist for me more richly and permanently than all the other Banffs…nor would I choose another place to live."

Among Whyte's early heroes were wilderness painter Carl Rungius and legendary outfitter Jimmy Simpson. Whyte's first creative project dedicated to the Rocky Mountains was the 1968 film *Jimmy Simpson, Mountain Man*.

In the early 1960s, Whyte studied writing at the University of Alberta and was a fixture in Edmonton's creative writing scene. Whyte also took an interest in publishing. In 1971, his publishing house, Summerthought Press, released *Canadian Rockies Trail Guide: A Hiker's Manual*, by Brian Patton and Bart Robinson. More than 30 years later, the book is in its seventh edition, has sold over 200,000 copies and is considered the bible for those hiking the Canadian Rockies.

Above all, Whyte was an avid and prolific writer. His poetry was often very visual, with words placed on the page in such a manner as to form foreground images, landscapes or mazes. In 1983, he became the first recipient of the Stephan Stephansson Award for Poetry for his much-acclaimed work *Homage, Henry Kelsey.* Apart from poetry, Whyte wrote or contributed to more than 20 books on the Rockies, many of them concerning the history of the region.

By all accounts, Whyte was well liked and personable. However, he also could use his tongue as a rapier when provoked. As president of the Writers' Guild of Alberta in 1991, it fell to Whyte to introduce then Culture minister Doug Main at the guild's annual banquet. Incensed that the Alberta government had refused financial aid to Hurtig Publishers and that the trail-blazing publishing house had subsequently folded, Whyte said sarcastically that the minister came from a family so well known that streets all over Alberta were named after it. He went on to say that he'd seen Hurtig's *Junior Canadian Encyclopedia* in the minister's office, but that it would likely do the minister more good if Main removed the shrink wrap.

Whyte certainly had strong opinions on a variety of subjects. In his weekly column in Banff's *Crag and Canyon* newspaper, he regularly railed against the commercialization of Banff, which he saw as destroying the charm, culture and history of the region.

In 1980, Whyte took over as curator of the Whyte Museum of the Canadian Rockies, founded 20 years earlier by his aunt and uncle, the artists Peter and Catherine Whyte. In his new role, he aggressively sought to continue the family commitment to preserving the heritage of Banff's pioneer past.

Jon Whyte died of cancer in 1992 at 51. The epitaph on the headstone of his grave is a fitting visual poem: the word "earth" repeated four times in a circle. The exuberance of Whyte's life touched all who knew him and that was clear in the posthumous praise and respect declared for him. Author Myrna Kostash wrote: "Of all the people I know, Jon was the one who most hugely enjoyed life —books, friends, conversation, wordplay, dictionaries, food, treks, beasts, ghosts, lore—so much so that his joy spilled over into the lives of any who drew near him."

Francis Winspear

Francis Winspear was certainly skilled at making money. At his peak, he owned or controlled dozens of large, successful businesses, and amassed well over $100 million in personal wealth. But it was his talent for giving that truly set him apart.

Winspear is best known as the man who contributed $6 million toward the construction of the Edmonton concert hall that now bears his name—the largest-ever single donation by an individual to a Canadian arts organization. He's also remembered as a gifted teacher and a brilliant businessman, who challenged and inspired everyone who worked with him.

Winspear was born in England in 1903 and moved to Alberta when he was seven. He grew up in the tiny hamlet of Namaka, about 65 kilometres east of Calgary, where his father ran the local general store. He graduated from high school at the age of 14, then took a job as a bank clerk for four years while studying accounting by correspondence.

In 1927 he married Bessie Brooks Watchorn, and together they had two sons, Claude and Bill.

After articling as an accountant, Winspear ran the Edmonton office of Peat, Marwick and Mitchel. He soon developed a reputation for spotting and hiring talented young accountants. Eventually, he opened his own firm, Winspear, Higgins, Stevenson and Doan.

Over the course of his business career, Winspear became famous for his ability to save failing businesses. He eventually controlled over 40 companies, many of which were central to Alberta's economic development. Among them were Premier Steel, the first steel plant in Alberta, and Gold Standard Oils, an early investor in the venture that would become Suncor. Winspear approached every relationship in his life, both personal and professional, with responsibility and respect.

No matter how busy he became, he always found time to volunteer. He served as president of both the Edmonton and the Canadian Chamber of Commerce. He sat on the Edmonton Symphony's board of directors and was a patron of a number of other arts organizations. He also maintained lifetime ties with the University of Alberta, first as an accounting professor in the 1920s, then as dean of the business school, and finally as Professor Emeritus and an ongoing donor.

In the 1950s, Winspear assembled the managers of his companies and asked them to design a continuing fund to support social welfare, the arts, medicine, education and other causes. They collectively decided that each company would contribute a fixed percentage of its profits to a foundation. Eventually, the Winspear Foundation became self-sustaining, and continues to make annual grants equal to the income it generates.

Bessie Winspear fell ill in the 1970s and died in 1979. The following year, Francis Winspear married Harriet Snowball, a long-time friend. The two spent their years together travelling, entertaining and spending time with their combined extended families. "Old age is fun," wrote Winspear, "even as finance and business were fun."

Although Winspear didn't survive to see the opening of the Francis Winspear Centre for Music, he was on hand in June 1995 to shovel concrete at the ceremonial start of construction.

After Winspear's death, in January 1997, his son Bill said, "He really felt he owed the community and he did his best to repay it." Judging by the enduring evidence, he did a pretty good job.

Index